CHILIS

CHILIS

HOW TO GROW, HARVEST, AND COOK WITH YOUR FAVORITE HOT PEPPERS

EVA ROBILD, TEXT
KERSTIN ROSENGREN, EXPERT KNOWLEDGE
PERNILLA BERGDAHL, PHOTO
GUN PENHOAT, TRANSLATION

Skyhorse Publishing

CHEW

A SEARING PASSION

IMAGINE BITING INTO a fresh and supple chili. Chew thoroughly! Feel the intense flavor on your tongue and then experience how the heat disperses within your mouth. The heat creeps up on you, drops of sweat bead on your upper lip and forehead, maybe even in your ears and around your eyes. Salivation increases, and if the chili is really hot you might get hiccups or start to cough. No other vegetable or fruit generates so many bodily reactions after just one single bite. Apart from the heat, you might make out a tropical sweetness, a bitter note or a hint of citrus—all depending on what kind of chili you've eaten. If it is too blisteringly hot you'll probably get up, catch your breath and search for something cool to drink.

Capsicum, the chili pepper, is a berry, botanically speaking. In the industry it is referred to as a fruit, and it is used as a vegetable. When dried, the chili is a spice. Maybe it sounds a bit complicated, but it is enough if you remember that when it comes to chili, it could mean a lot of things.

Chili has caused sensations for thousands of years and is adored in many parts of the world. Chili is probably the commercial product quickest to establish itself all over the globe—chili was everywhere long before its name was known. Chili is an integral part of the daily life of billions of people, a spice that adds vitamins and flavors to foodstuffs for even the most destitute people. Once chilis were "discovered" by Columbus at the end of the 15th century, they quickly made their way from South and Central America to Europe and on to Asia, the Middle East, and Africa, where just as quickly they assimilated to many countries' culinary culture.

Famous Swedish botanist Carl von Linné mentions chili for the first time in 1749, when he visited the cultivations in a field in Limhamn, on the outskirts of the southern Swedish town of Malmö. However, there are no reliable records of how common it was in Swedish kitchens in the 18th century. There is no mention of chilis in the cookbooks of that era, but red long pepper might have been alluded to, probably in reference to chili, since a true (Indian) long pepper is dark brown and is more reminiscent of black pepper. What is known, however, is that chili appeared relatively early in the apothecary inventory as a medicinal herb.

The Swedes' knowledge of different species of chilies and their usage is surprisingly narrow—for instance, many recipes still call for one to two red or green chili fruits to be added to a stew. This doesn't necessarily mean that chefs don't know any of the chilies' names; it might just refer to the meager offerings in the way of fresh chilies in grocery stores. As recently as 10 years ago, you could thank your lucky stars if you found these red and green chilies at the supermarket; however, lately fresh jalapeños, habaneros and sometimes even the superhot Trinidad Moruga Scorpion and Carolina Reaper have made an appearance on grocery shelves.

You beget a considerably larger choice of species and varieties to use in cooking if you grow your own chilies, and can select among hundreds of tasty varieties. The book's expert and well-versed chili-grower Kerstin Rosengren from Glemmingebro on Österlen (in the southern Swedish province of Skåne), lives with chilies year-round, and grows at least 300 different varieties each year. Growing chilies demands commitment and interest, and those of you who learn how to do it will be richly rewarded.

The best thing about chilis is the amazing variety out there. There is everything from the mildest types, which are close to bell peppers in taste, to those so hot your whole body catches fire after just a teeny, tiny bite. Chilis are probably the world's most beautiful fruit, and not just those as red as a freshly painted Ferrari, but also thanks to their different shapes and their large range of colors, from creamy white and yellow to green, orange, lilac, and as black as a vegetable can ever get.

You can grow chilis because of their beauty, because they are delicious, because they are hot, because you like to cook, or simply because you relish a real challenge—or a combination of all of the above.

If you feel perspiration on your upper lip or around your eyes merely from reading about chilis, you're not alone. This book's author sweated profusely in front of the screen while working on this book.

However, the wonderful thing about chilis isn't just all the ways in which they heat things up, but that they also provide a jolt of endorphins. Endorphins are the body's own morphine, a pain reliever

as well as a stimulant—yes, you quite simply might experience a "chili high" that is slightly addictive. We want to strengthen your passion for chilis by sharing our knowledge.

Welcome to our sizzling hot world!
Eva, Kerstin, and Pernilla

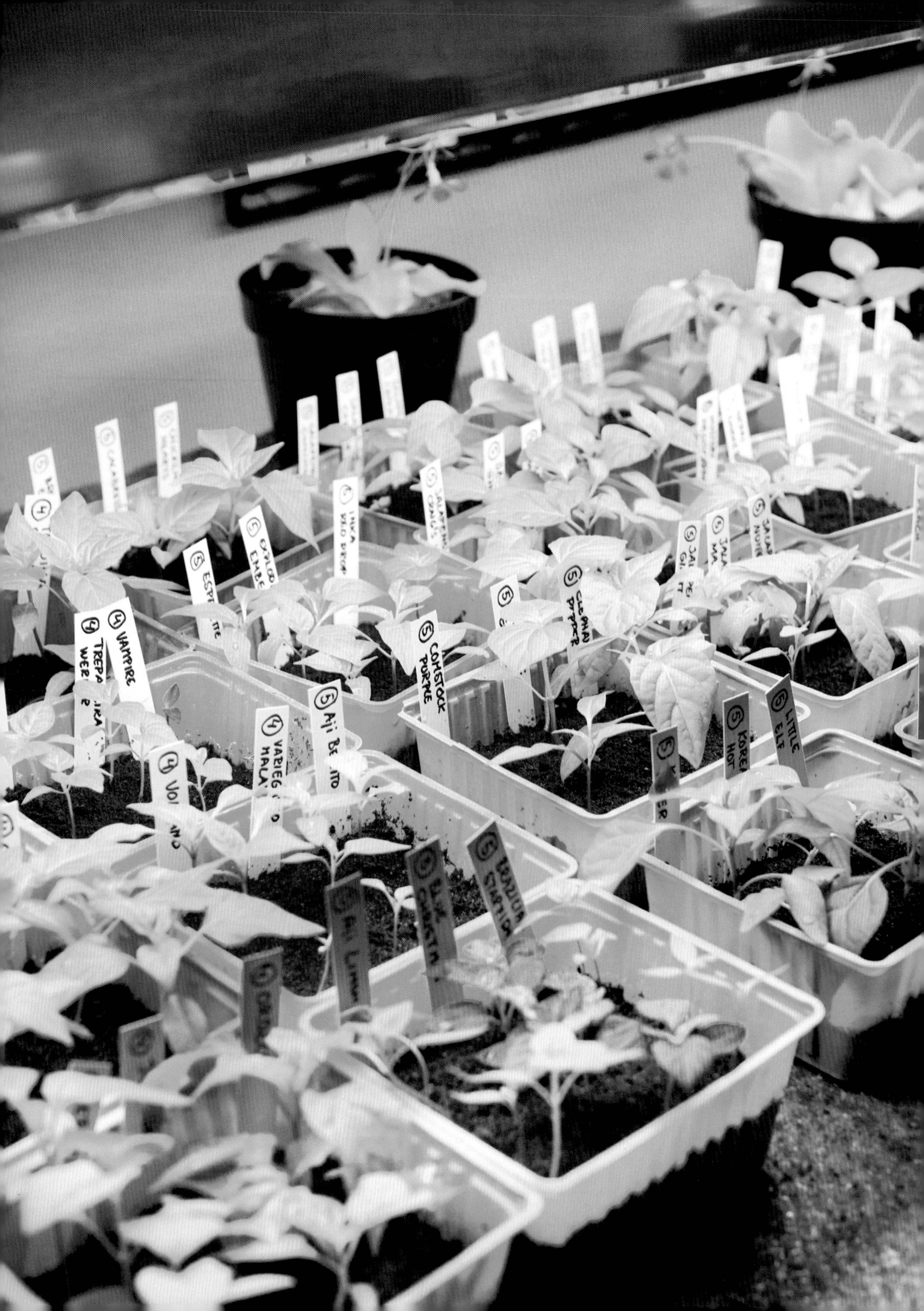
4 VAMPIRE
5 COMSTOCK PURPLE
5 LITTLE ELF

GROW

FROM SEED TO HARVEST

TRINITY 7

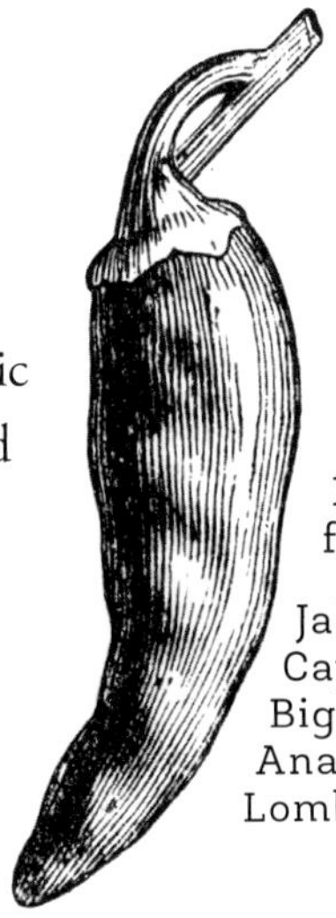

Easy to grow for beginners:

Jalapeño
Cayenne Golden
Big Jim
Anaheim
Lombardo

MAKING A SEED grow is a little like performing a magic trick; under your care a dry, small seed is transformed into something living and growing—a plant! When the seed is provided with warmth and water the growing process begins. What it will become is already predestined in the seed's genes. It isn't just decided that it will become a plant of the family Capsicum, but also whether it is to become a habanero or jalapeño, or whichever type you sowed.

Well-known chili varieties are sold in plant nurseries and at several larger and smaller seed companies online. Vendors who sell seeds as a main product must guarantee the purity of the seeds as well as a certain germination rate to be permitted to sell the seeds. You can be confident when buying from them, because you know what you're getting and that the seeds will grow. Sometimes you might get lucky and find organic seeds that have been produced without the use of chemical fertilizers or pesticides. Seed packets labeled F1 mean that these are first generation seeds from select plants. They have especially good properties in looks, flavor, and/or cultivation (they're less susceptible to disease, for example). An F1 hybrid will seldom make a stable seed, so it's not a good idea to collect those seeds. If you want to find unusual varieties, try vendor websites from other countries.

IT IS BETTER TO SOW EARLY

To succeed in your cultivation and to grow ripe fruits, it is advisable to always start the chili plants indoors (pre-cultivate). As chili plants require a long growing season, the frost-free months aren't enough, not even if you grow them in a greenhouse. In our experience, the more practical way to do it is to sow the seeds as early as in fall or early winter, and place them in a greenhouse over spring or early summer. That way the plants can benefit from natural light and summer heat.

The different species develop at different speeds from seed to harvest, varying from about 120 and 300 days. The species *C. pubescens*, the Rocoto chili and *C. chinense*, the Havana pepper, have the longest development from seed to fruit, and you need to sow them first, preferably as early as October–November. Chili varieties that belong to the species *C. annuum*, the Spanish chili, *C. baccatum*, the berry chili fruit, and *C. frutescens*, the Tabasco chili, can be sown later, but typically no later than February.

If you sow early, your harvest can begin as early as May–June and continue until the first frost (or longer, if you move your plants inside the house in the fall). One advantage of early sowing is that you can start harvesting earlier and thus not have to move large, space-needy plants full of unripe fruit inside the house in the fall. If you want to grow them in garden beds, it is also important to sow them early to transplant out large plants. This increases the likelihood of a harvest of ripe fruit, even taking into account our short summers. Early sowing demands extra light; read more about lighting on the next page.

If you can create optimal conditions with heat, water, and light, there's nothing stopping you from growing chilis all year.

GERMINATION

The seeds germinate after 6–10 days, but sometimes it can take several weeks. If you want to provide seeds with the best conditions for germinating quickly, place sowings where it is warm, preferably in a place that it is between 77°F–86°F (25°C–30°C). The simplest way to do this is to get a heating mat or a sowing box with a built-in thermostat that stays at the correct temperature. You can also place the sowing box on a floor with subfloor heating or on a hot, under-window heater. A sheet of plastic film or a lid placed over the sowing facilitates germination, but don't forget to make air holes to allow for proper ventilation.

The reason for slow seed germination might depend on the species, but also on old seeds and that the seeds may have entered "seed dormancy." Place the sown seed in a warmer place, maintain even moisture, and have patience! Non-germination might also be because the soil was left to dry out after germination had begun, making it impossible to wake the seed up again. If it is too wet or cold, or both, the seeds might have rotted, at which point it's all over for them.

LIGHTING

During the dark season (October–March) the chili plants need light to grow well. It is especially important to provide early sown seed plants with adequate light to make them grow nice and sturdy, which also makes them hardier.

There is a wide assortment of good grow lights in plant nurseries, but make sure that the setup isn't too low, since you must be able to move the lights up as the plants grow. The best is to hang the lights from the ceiling and move the light up and down as needed. A good distance between the light source and the plant is approximately 6 to 8 inches (15–30 cm.). The leaves might burn if the lights are closer. The best light sources provide lots of light but generate little heat.

Jonas Bergström at Instutitionen för Biosystem och teknology (The Institute for Biosystems and Technology) at the consulting firm ELU has looked closer at how plants react to light, and says that white light is best—independent of light source—and recommends 100–200 watt per 10¾ sq ft (1 sq meter) when forcing plants, and 50–100 watt for overwintering plants. Lamps with blue/red light sold as growth lights have a positive effect on photosynthesis. For example, the red light encourages increased root development and more side shoots. However the difference between these lights and regular lights is so marginal that these lamps are not needed for hobby growers. Red and blue lights can be uncomfortable in a home, and it is more difficult to see how the plants are doing because it is impossible to see the color of the leaves when the lights are on. In any case, as white light contains the full spectrum of light, the plants get what they need. It is also pleasant to look at and is therefore preferable inside a dwelling. Strip lights are cheap to buy and to run. Kerstin, who forces hundreds of plants, needs lighting covering large areas, so she uses industrial fixtures with reflectors that are attached to the ceiling with chains. The lights can be raised as the plants grow. The light source is strip lights with a color temperature of 4,100 kelvin, i.e., a cold white light that mimics daylight. If you prefer to use LED strip lights, choose a T5 39W High Output strip light, for example. Your plants also get daylight if they're positioned near a window—even if it is quite a small amount during winter—while in a dark basement you'll have to hang up some extra lights. If you're panic-stricken from all the technical terms, you can calm yourself by remembering that a lighted desk lamp above the growing seeds is better than nothing, as long as it doesn't generate too much heat and burn the leaves.

Strip-light fixtures are an economical way to provide plants with good growth light.

The light should be turned on between 12–16 hours every 24 hours. Turning off the light at night provides the plants with a natural rhythm, and they can grow between the day's photosynthesis and the night's cell respiration.

HYBRIDS AND SEED CULTIVATION

Chili plants are self-pollinating, which means that they don't need another flower to produce fruit. Cross-pollination occurs when insects transport pollen from a flower's stamen to the stigma of another flower; the result can be seeds which, in the next generation, grow fruits that are different in looks, taste, and strength.

There might be a lack of insects when cultivation happens inside, so you might need to pollinate by shaking the plant or by carrying the pollen between plants using a watercolor paintbrush.

It might be tempting to sow seeds from a fruit you've bought at the grocery store. Maybe you'll get a fruit that is like the one you bought, but that is not a sure thing by a long shot! It might have been an F1-type, or perhaps the fruit was cross-pollinated with an unknown species, and so you might end up with something completely different from what you expected. It is better to buy your seeds from an established seed seller if you want to be sure that the plant you lavish with care gives you what you want.

Find out if the seeds come from plants that were isolated when you exchange seeds with friends or other growers, or you risk getting a completely different chili than the one you bargained for. If you buy so-called 'freely pollinated' chilis, cross-pollination is very likely.

If you want to grow your own seeds and be sure that the variety stays "true," that it retains all its properties, you must keep the plant segregated so no insect cross-pollinates it with pollen from another specimen. The best way to guarantee true seeds is to isolate a few flowers while they're already budding. You could attach a bag (small plastic jewelry bags work perfectly here) over the bud, for instance.

Once the flower is in bloom, shake the branch with the flower to make the pollen move from stamen to stigma on the (same) flower, i.e., self-pollination. You can remove the bag when the fruit begins to develop after a few weeks, and then attach a label so you know which fruit contains the "true" seeds.

Remember that the fruits need to be completely ripe before you harvest their seeds. A green or unripe fruit will seldom have viable seeds. It is especially important to be careful with species that usually are eaten when green, such as Padrón peppers. Seeds from chilis that are dried in high heat hardly ever germinate.

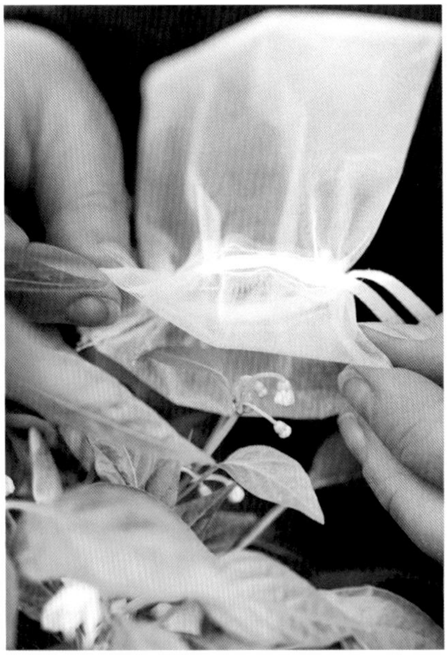

You can attach a bag (small plastic jewelry bags work fine) over the flower bud to guarantee that the plant provides true seeds.

HARVEST SEEDS

Harvest attractive fruit that are typical of the plant variety, without any insect damage or plant disease. It needs to be ripe, edging on overripe, dry and slightly wrinkly. Open the fruit and cut off the seeds from the seed fastenings/inner part of the fruit. Place the seeds in, say, a coffee filter to dry. Don't forget to label the filter! You can put the seeds, once they are thoroughly dry, in a plastic resealable bag or in a seed envelope. Store the seeds in a dry and dark place. At room temperature the seeds will remain viable for 3–4 years. If you want to keep them longer, store them in a cool environment, such as in a refrigerator or freezer.

YOUR OWN HYBRIDS

Try making your own chili varieties! Isolate a plant (the mother plant) from the other chili plants (or place a plastic bag over the buds). When a bud is in flower, immediately cut off all the stamens so there can be no self-pollination. Then you take pollen from another (also isolated) plant and bring it using a cotton tip to the mother plant's stigma. By all means, pollinate several flowers on the mother plant, since it is not a given that they all will take. Then isolate the flowers until fruits start to develop. When the fruits are ripe, harvest the seeds, and you'll see the result when you sow next season. If you get fine fruits, save the seeds. A chili has to grow true over several seasons and show itself to be stable, and that it keeps its qualities from year to year, in order to be accepted as a new variety.

It's fine to sow seeds from dried chilis, as long as they were dried at room temperature.

SOWING: STEP-BY-STEP

1. Use clean pots, such as low sowing boxes for wide sowing.
2. Layer the bottom of the pot with ¾"–1¼" (2–3 cm.) organic soil.
3. Top with ⅓" (1 cm.) potting soil.
4. Dampen the soil slightly by misting it with a spray bottle.
5. Sow in rows, leaving ½"–¾" (1½ cm.–2 cm.) between the seeds.
6. Add a name tag for each kind of pepper.
7. Press the seed down into the potting soil about ⅕" (½ cm.).
8. Spray again to dampen the soil.
9. Cover the sowed seeds with a plastic lid or sheet of plastic wrap, if you wish.
10. Place the sowed seeds in a warm place. Optimal temperature is 77°F–86°F (25°C–30°C).

THE SPROUT IS PEEKING THROUGH

A great moment for every chili grower is when the season's first sprout peeks up through the soil. First it looks like a small green loop or small bent back, but only a few hours later the stalk will have straightened up and the first leaves unfolded. The seed contains everything it needs—the endosperm—for it to grow, develop its first root, sprout, and develop first leaves. These first leaves are called cotyledons, and their main function is to begin photosynthesis to allow the plant to start converting carbon dioxide, water, and light to carbohydrates and oxygen, which are needed for the plant to continue to grow. Sometimes the seed husk is still stuck to the seed, which prevents the leaves from unfolding. If you shower the sprout a few times the husk usually falls off. When the chili's "real" characteristic plant leaves develop, the cotyledons wither since their work is now done.

The plant is very fragile when it still only has one pair of leaves, and it only needs water and light. At this point, applying a fertilizer that's too strong might scorch the leaves, or in the worst-case scenario, kill the plant. Wait to fertilize when it is time to repot it.

Once the plants have reached this size, repot them in their own individual pots.

OTHER WAYS TO SOW

As chili seeds can go dormant and need to be "woken" in order to germinate, many experiment with more or less weird ways to encourage quicker germination. Chili enthusiasts who spread these "tips" on their websites or in YouTube videos are often convinced of their advice's excellence. Try them if you like, but we have not noticed any difference.

Soak the seed in water for 12–24 hours before sowing. This is a lot of work for weak results. It might be worth trying if the seeds are more than 3 years old.

Soak the seed in 3% potassium nitrate 6 days before sowing. A lot of bother, rather iffy from an organic perspective, and Kerstin got worse results than when sowing the conventional way.

Soak the seed in water mixed with baking powder (2/5 tsp to scant ¼ cup water) for 12–24 hours before sowing. Avoid baking powder if you want to grow organic crops.

Keep the sowed seeds at 86°F (30°C) temperature for 18 hours; lower to 59°F (15°C) for 6 hours and then raise the temperature to 86°F (30°C) again. Lots of unnecessary work, since an even temperature of approximately 77°F (25°C) provides good results.

Place the seed in 77°F (25°C)–86°F (30°C) tea for about 5 minutes before sowing (water the sowed seed with the rest of the tea). Unnecessary work for a weak result.

Rub the seed's surface with sand before sowing (to rough up the surface). The seeds run the risk of breaking since they are very fragile.

Sow the seeds in rooting or grow plugs instead of soil. A good method if you prefer doing it this way. It is very important to not let the plugs dry out!

Place the seeds on damp paper towels; keep them in a plastic bag on top of a warm heater until the seeds have sprouted, and then place them in the soil. A lot of fuss, and the risk is that the sprout will dry up if you're not very vigilant.

CARE OF THE SEED PLANTING

The seed plantings should be checked several times daily. It is of utmost importance to keep the soil evenly damp. It should absolutely never be left to dry out, but should not be too wet, either. dried-out or rotted seed can't be revived. If you have covered the planting with a lid or plastic wrap, it is time to remove it once the seed has sprouted.

If you haven't set up a grow light right from the start, it is time to do this as soon as the seed has sprouted. The earlier the plant gets extra light, the better. The goal is for it to become a solid and sturdy plant, which is achieved through light and heat. Not enough light makes plants spindly and weak that will easily tip over, and are also more likely to suffer damage when repotted and moved. The worst combination is too little light and too much heat, because the plants shoot up very tall and become both easily damaged and difficult to handle. By being in good grow light and a somewhat lowered temperature—about 64.4°F (18°C)—the plants have the best conditions to become sturdy and plump. However, the final height of the plant is determined by the genes of the species, and can vary between 8" (20 cm.) and six and a half feet (2 meters).

Chili plants don't need to be pruned or trimmed back; they don't develop quicker or branch out more when pruned. The only result is that fruiting is delayed. Certain species of chilis, especially of C. *baccatum*, will grow very straggly, in which case you can prune the branches that stick out too much. Overwintered plants can be pruned in January–February to stimulate them and encourage new growth. Read more about overwintering on page 37. The tops with soft stems can be used as cuttings for new plants. Keep 2–3 leaves and put the cuttings into aerated soil. They need to be kept in the light and on a heated surface to be able to take root.

REPOTTING

Once the plants have grown 2–4 true leaves, i.e., leaves characteristic of the chili plant, it is time for the first repotting. No harm done if the plant has grown a few more leaves, but don't wait too long because the plant will slow down its growth. The pot needs to be big enough to allow the plant to grow substantially and develop a strong root system before the next repotting. A 3½" (9 cm.) diameter pot is enough. Repotting is done once or twice more, depending on the growth of the plant. When the roots poke out of the hole at the bottom of the pot, it is time to move the plant into a pot just slightly larger than the old one. The final pot, the one the plant will spend the entire season in, should be at least 11¾" in diameter, and contain between 7 and 8 quarts of soil. You can add some more fertilizer than at the first repotting, but remember not to put it directly against the roots, which could get damaged and burned by the salts in the fertilizer.

The plants might require a support stake once they have reached a height of 9¾"–11¾" (25 cm.–30 cm.). You push it into the pot and tie it around the plant's stem. If the plant buds early on, pick off the early flower to encourage the plant to develop further.

REPOTTING STEP-BY-STEP

1. Get a pot 3½" (9 cm.) in diameter (for the second repotting, use a 6"–7¾" [15 cm.–7¾"]-diameter pot, and for third repotting, an approximately 11¾" (30 cm.)-diameter pot).

2. Fill one fourth of the pot with organic soil. Kerstin uses professional grower's soil, which contains added basalt rock dust.

3. Add manure. Kerstin uses a mix of 1 tsp chicken manure, 1 tsp Epsom salt, ½ tsp neem seed meal and ½ tsp bat guano. Increase these amounts a little at subsequent repottings.

4. Fill up with soil until about ¾" below the pot's edge.

5. Dig a hole in the soil and carefully lift a chili plant in, with a spoon for example.

6. Place the plant in the hole and press down so it is firmly anchored. Plant deep, preferably, leaving about 1/5" to ¼" (1/2 cm. to 1 cm.) between soil and the first true leaves, since the plant will develop roots on the stem below the soil's surface.

7. Label each pot.

NUTRITION

• BASALT ROCK DUST •
This is volcanic rock that has been milled to the consistency of flour. It contains many different minerals that strengthen the plants and provides more nutritional fruits.
Use: Mixed into the soil or is mixed into the soil surface.
Dosage: 1 quart (1 liter) per 50 quarts (50 liters) of soil
Where to buy: At some garden nurseries and online.

• CHICKEN MANURE •
This is manure from chickens; it is often sold as pellets. This is a fertilizer with a high nitrogen content, which promotes growth and is therefore used for plant forcing and early in the season.
Usage: Mixed into the soil or is dissolved in water and watered in.
Dosage: 1–2 tbsp per quart of soil or ¼ cup (½ dl.) per 5 quarts (5 liters) of water.
Where to buy: Garden centers and home improvement stores

• EPSOM SALT •
This is magnesium sulfate, also called Epsom or bitter salt. It frees up other nutrients in the soil, improves seed germination, strengthens the plant and the chlorophyll production, and improves the plants uptake of phosphorus and nitrogen.
Usage: Mixes into the soil at planting time, or dissolved in water and watered in.
Dosage: 1–2 tbsp per 1 quart soil or 1 tbsp per 5 quart (5 liters) water.
Where to buy: Mostly online.

• NEEM SEED MEAL •
Seed milled from the fruit and seeds from the neem tree. It contains nitrogen, phosphorus and potassium, plus many minerals. The nitrogen is dispersed slowly, making it long acting. Neem is considered plant strengthening, and helps reduce the risk for soil-borne diseases and pest attacks.
Usage: It is mixed directly into the soil or dissolved in water and watered in.
Dosage: ½–1 tsp per 1 quart (1 liter) soil or ½ tbsp per 1 quart (1 liter) water
Where to buy: Mostly online.

• BAT GUANO •
This is bat excrement. It's a strong fertilizer with high phosphorus content that promotes healthy soil microorganisms, which in turn strengthen and protect the plant.
Usage: This is mixed into the soil or dissolved in water and watered in.
Dosage: ½ tbsp per 1 quart (1 liter) soil or 1 tbsp per 5 quart (5 liter) water.
Where to buy: Garden centers and online.

• FISH MIX •
This is fish emulsion mixed with sugar beet extract. Increases growth and promotes healthy soil microorganisms.
Usage: This is dissolved in water and watered in.
Dosage: ⅖–1 tsp per 1 quart (1 liter) water.
Where to buy: Garden centers and online.

• SEAWEED •
This is kelp extract. It stimulates growth and strengthens the plant, and promotes healthy microorganisms and mycorrhiza (natural occurring fungal thread) in the soil.
Uses: This is dissolved in water and watered in.
Dosage: ⅖ tsp per 1 quart (1 liter) water.
Where to buy: Garden centers and online.

You can also buy forced plants if you don't want, or don't have the opportunity, to start plants from seed. Selections in garden centers are usually largest in April–May. Buy sturdy, healthy plants, and why not try organically grown plants?

Fertilize the chili plants throughout the entire season. This is critical for good growth and fruiting. Start fertilizing by adding nutrients to the soil as soon as you do the first repotting. The added nutrition in the soil lasts between 4–8 weeks. After that runs out, begin watering the plants with a weak fertilizer solution at each watering (check the table for dosage). This gives them even and steady access to nutrition, which lowers the risk of root burn—a reality you will face if you fertilize heavily but not often enough. Once the plants have moved into the greenhouse in spring, they should be fertilized 3–4 times a week with a liquid fertilizer. It's a good idea to vary between Epsom salt, fish mix, and seaweed fertilizer. Bat guano and chicken manure are not used past midsummer, since too much nitrogen late in the season produces lots of leaves but less fruit.

HOW TO CHOOSE SOIL

Go for well-known, reputable brands of potting and planting soil, and try to find organic soil. The soil sold in garden centers is made up primarily (85%) of peat; sand, clay and nutrients in varying amounts are also added; sometimes Leca balls are incorporated, which provide better drainage. Kerstin has tried many different soils as well as different types of fertilizers, and is of the opinion that it is not the soil you choose that is the main concern, but that you fertilize the soil when potting up and continue to do so throughout the growing season. Kerstin also adds 1 quart (1 liter) basalt rock flour to each 50-quart (50-liter) bag of soil, because in her experience this strengthens the plant and promotes good growth.

When spring arrives, it is time at last to move the pots into the greenhouse. A frost sensor keeps an eye on the temperature.

MOVING-OUT TIME

When you have potted up the chili plants a few times and they have reached a height of about 11¾"–15¾" (30 cm.–40 cm.), the greenhouse usually starts to lack space. If the plants are very crowded they will also start competing for light and tend to reach upward, which can result in tall and gangly plants. The plants stay lower and sturdier if placed further apart. Chili plants are perfect to grow in greenhouses, polytunnels, or on a glassed-in porch/balcony, as they love sun and heat. The plants are very sensitive to the cold, so don't move them outside too early. They are especially delicate in early spring when they are used to an inside environment.

The 300 different chili varieties that Kerstin grows every year need daily care to grow well, stay healthy, and provide a good harvest.

PESTS AND FUNGI

Chili plants contain a lot of carbohydrates, which easily attracts insects. Not many people have grown chilis without also having the plants attacked by pests. Therefore it is important to prevent infestations. The first step is to provide the plants with proper amounts of water and fertilizer. A dried-out, overwatered, or enfeebled plant is more susceptible to insect damage. It's also important to practice good plant hygiene, i.e. to remove yellowed and withered leaves from the plant and soil, as well as the windowsills.

The plants are better protected against infestation if they are sprayed with neem oil every other week. Neem oil is sold as leaf shine in Sweden, but is an allowed pesticide in the United States and other countries. Neem oil is extracted from the neem tree, *Azadirachta indica*, and is a plant-based product that contains elements that confuse pests and prevent them from eating, mating, and laying eggs. Spraying the plants with an Epsom salt solution is another way to strengthen the plants' resilience, primarily against fungal diseases.

HOW TO TREAT A PEST INFESTATION

Don't panic when you discover pests on your plants! The worst is usually removed by spraying the plant with water. Avoid poison and homemade remedies made from cigarette butts or other dangerous substances that will be absorbed by the plants. Chilis are edibles!

<u>Fungus gnats</u> are tiny flies that "bumble" around the plants and lay their eggs in the soil. The eggs then become larvae and chew on the roots. Prevent this by keeping the soil's surface dry. Carnivorous plants "catch" the flies, as does yellow flypaper (sold wherever insecticides are sold). The larvae can be fought with nematodes.

<u>Aphids</u> suck the sap out of the plant and make it weak. Occasional insects can be squeezed between the fingers, but a larger infestation can be treated with a strong jet of water. Be careful not to damage the plant leaves. Follow this with neem oil spray for three days. An effective treatment is to use parasitic insects that live on aphids. You buy them alive, on the internet, and they arrive by mail. The aphids have to be present already as the parasites lay their eggs in the aphid, which swells into a tiny cocoon. This hatches after a few weeks and starts to hunt for aphids. It's often enough to set out one lot of parasite insects in the spring to be protected against aphids the entire season. The parasites can be used indoors, on porches, and in greenhouses. Remember that they are alive and need to be set out immediately after they arrive.

<u>Whiteflies</u> are tiny white lice that disperse in a cloud when you approach. They suck the sap out of the plant. Yellow fly-paper and carnivorous plants can catch some of the whiteflies. Parasitic insects work on whiteflies, too, but you might have to wait up to 4 weeks to see any results. Remember that you need a different parasitic insect for whiteflies, not the same as for aphids.

<u>Spider mites</u> are usually greenhouse mites, pinhead-sized green or red mites that suck on the leaves and leave white marks. After a while a white spiderweb-like weave is formed. False spider mites are even tinier and suck on the leaves, making them turn yellow with the network of nerves appearing in green. Both types of mites are treated with soapy water or beneficial insects, i.e., different types of parasitic spider mites.

Spider mites

Blossom end rot

Aphids

You can try to prune an established plant hard if the infestation is very serious. A new stem and leaves will have grown out after about 2 months, and if it is early in the season the plant will have time to set fruit, even if the harvest will be later. However, this is not recommended for healthy plants.

<u>Scale</u> looks like brown spots often situated on the stem and along the leaf nerves on the underside of the leaves. Dip a cotton Q-tip in methylated spirit and dab it on each scale to kill it. It works well, too, to spray with soapy water mixed with methylated spirit (1 quart [1 liter] water, 1 tbsp carbolic soap, 1 tbsp methylated spirit). Repeat weekly until the infestation is gone. Mealybugs are treated the same way.

<u>Blossom-end rot</u> is a fungal disease that shows up as brown, soft spots on the fruit. The disease is the result of a lack of calcium or uneven watering. Prevent blossom-end rot by fertilizing well and adding extra nutrients when needed.

If you're growing outside in a pot, choose a warm, sunny spot that is protected from the wind. Here you can see, among others, Habanero Orange, Apache, and Basket of Fire.

The earlier the plants can move outside, the better they will fare. When they receive a natural variation between day and night temperatures and more natural light, they become sturdier and healthier. But if the plants are to be moved out to the greenhouse already in March–April, you'll need a fan with a thermostat that heats the greenhouse to the desired temperature, i.e., 50°F (10°C) both day and night. Plastic Bubble Wrap attached to the ceiling, or a mini greenhouse/tent made of Bubble Wrap, minimizes heat loss.

If you can't heat your greenhouse, the move outside will have to wait until night frosts are past in May–June and the greenhouse temperature is at least 50°F (10°C) at night, and preferably twice that during the day.

The plants need to be hardened off if they are going to stay outside during the summer; they need to get used to the outside climate. At first they must be protected from not only the cold, but also from wind, rain, and sunshine. Put the plants outside when the temperature is at least 50°F (10°C), preferably when it is overcast and there's no wind. It won't hurt to cover them with a fiber cloth for extra protection. Leave the plants outside for short periods to start with, and increase the time span a little each day until the risk of night frost is past and the plants can move outside.

SUMMER CARE

Summer is the time for the chili plants to grow, flower, and set fruit. They manage this very well on their own as long as you provide water and nutrients. The smaller pots the plants grow in, the more you will have to water them. However, if the pots are too large for the plants, it might be difficult to judge the right amount of watering needed. It is a bit of an art to learn how to water just right; practice makes perfect. The plants need a certain amount of moisture, but the soil needs to dry a little between watering. Soil that's too wet will lack oxygen, and the roots will atrophy.

Watering about every other day is a good benchmark, but some plants will require more frequent watering, others less. How often and how much you water will depend on the weather, the plants' size, and the amount of soil in the pot. Push a finger into the soil if you're unsure, and feel, because only checking the surface is not a good guide. After

GROW EVERYWHERE

GROW INDOORS

If you grow indoors you can more or less grow all year—as long as you have access to really good lighting. You'll need to wait until February or March to sow seeds, or buy pre-forced plants in spring, if you grow on a windowsill without any extra light source. Make sure it doesn't get too hot in the window during hot summer days—you might need to cover the window with an extra drape in the middle of the day. Keep a close eye on signs of pests, as they thrive indoors. Preferably choose ornamental chilis that are both beautiful and tasty.

1. Malawi Birdseye
2. Aurora
3. Purple Tiger
4. Tricolor Variegata
5. Filius Blue

GROW ON THE BALCONY

Chilis grow fine on a balcony, but you must ensure that they get at least six hours, preferably more, of sunshine a day. They need this for fruit to develop optimally. Choose varieties of *C. annuum*, Spanish pepper, which ripens earlier and is therefore good to start with. Harden off the plants before you move them outside. Be prepared that a cold and rainy summer will provide an inferior outcome to one from a warm and sunny season.

1. Rooster Spurs
2. Apache
3. Jellybean
4. Jalapeño Cracked
5. Criolla de Coccina

HYDROPONIC GROWING

You can grow chilis totally without soil! Many have had success growing their chilis in closed water systems, also called hydroponic cultivation. The plants grow in a cube of rock wool or equivalent material, with automatic drip irrigation and fertilizing. DWC—deep water culture—is another water-based growing system. It works even on the balcony and doesn't require a pump.

1. Jimmy Nardello
2. Sarit Gat
3. Santa Fe Grande
4. Piment d'Espelette
5. Nepal Snakebite

It is easier to accommodate lower-growing varieties like Peruvian Purple, Aurora and Hungarian Hot Wax in an apartment.

a while you'll also be able to tell by the weight of the pot whether the soil is damp or dry. Lift and decide! A drooping plant might be a sign of drought, but also of overwatering or excess heat—the latter easily happens in a closed greenhouse. At temperatures above 86°F (30°C) the plant might stop growing and the flowers can drop off. Don't forget to practice good plant hygiene—continually remove withered leaves and treat for pests that appear. Add fertilizer as you water, 3–4 times a week, according to the table on page 25. Lack of nutrition usually shows up as puny growth or yellow leaves.

TOWARD SEASON'S END

Chili flowers are beautiful and vary both in size and color. The fruits develop quickly, from pinhead-sized green "marbles" to bigger and bigger fruits. They start out green but then they shift into red or yellow. Some varieties go through several color stages and can become black, lilac, orange, and beige on their way to full ripeness.

Padrón, poblano, and jalapeño are examples of chilis that are often harvested unripe, while they are still green. Many other varieties can, of course, also be used when green—if you want to pickle fefferoni (the Italians call them peperoni, the Italian name for chili), say, or slice them to add to a stew or a salad. Unripe fruit are, as a rule, slightly more bitter and milder, as fruitiness and heat don't develop fully until later in the ripening process.

The plants are usually full of fruit by the time daylight starts to diminish in September–October. The very best is to let the fruit fully ripen on the plant, as that is the way it reaches full potential both in flavor and in heat. If at all possible, move the plant to a frost-free spot on a heated porch, or indoors, so the fruits can ripen without being damaged by frost.

If it isn't possible to move the plants indoors in the fall, you can harvest the fruit and place them on a tray to ripen over time. Some types ripen well, while others remain green. The riper the fruits are when you harvest them, the greater the odds they will fully ripen after being harvested. It is said that ripening can be hastened if you place the chilis together with an apple.

OVERWINTERING PLANTS

All species of chilis are perennial, even if their growing ability might diminish after a few years. However, they cannot survive outdoors in the Scandinavian climate, and the plants have to be moved indoors in plenty of time before the first killing frost if you wish to overwinter them. Then you can continue to grow them on the windowsill or in a growing room outfitted with extra grow lights. Moving the plants indoors doesn't require the same care as moving them outside in the spring, but a climate change will still stress them. The air indoors is drier and warmer than they are used to, and they don't feel the temperature variations between warm days and cool nights, which they are used to from the greenhouse or on the balcony. They often react by dropping leaves, yellowing leaves, or drooping. Be careful to not overwater them. The fewer leaves on the plant, the smaller amount of water it needs. They usually appreciate a shower, though. If you prune the plant due to lack of space, it will need even less water. Continue to fertilize, but with a weak dose, throughout winter. It might also be a good thing to pinch off the flowers during the darkest months to direct growth strength to the plant and not to fruit production.

The chili plants need to stand in a light window in winter to receive as much light as possible. Preferably keep an extra grow light lit for 12–16 hours a day. Keep an eye out for pests, which easily follow the plants indoors. Prevent infestation by spraying the plants with neem oil. Overwintered plants can be pruned in January–February and be potted up in fresh soil at the same time of the year.

Keep a record so you know what you've sowed, when you sowed, how you watered and fertilized, and what the result has been from each different species and variety. Don't forget to move the plant labels, too, when you repot! These notes constitute invaluable knowledge for your next year's season start.

PEPPER PALACE
CHILI
THE KID
HOT SAUCE

LEARN

HISTORY AND POPULAR CULTURE

Langer Indianischer Pfeffer.

CCCCXIX.

It's not easy to get a clear idea of the true origin of the chili fruit, as it is partly hidden in the South American jungle. In 2007, Linda Perry, a botanical archaeologist, and her colleagues from the Smithsonian National Museum of Natural History presented proof that chilis have been cultivated from as far back as 7,000 to 9,000 years ago. She places the chilis' wild origin in Bolivia, Brazil, and other countries around the Andes in South America. Fossil traces at dwelling places show that chili cultivation existed in southwestern Ecuador more than 6,000 years ago. The indigenous populations of South America, such as the Aztec and Incas, also used chili for medicinal and religious purposes.

Traces in the Bahamas show that chili was there several thousands of years before Columbus arrived in the Americas, and archaeological digs in Mexico also prove that the chili has been grown there for more than 6,000 years. Archaeological finds from caves in Puebla and Tamaulipas indicate that cultivation of *C. annuum* began in Mexico; wild chili species and at least seven different varieties of Spanish pepper were cultivated. Microscopic chili remains in cooking vessels show clearly that chilis were consumed together with, among other things, corn, squash and beans. These are not wild chilis but cultivated varieties, because the area is too far from where the wild chilis grow, and the fruits are considerably larger than those of their wild counterparts. Archaeologists have also dug out very old traces of *C. frutescens* and *C. chinense* together with ceramic artifacts, which are believed to have been used in religious ceremonies. Researchers believe that Roccoto chili, *C. pubescens*, was domesticated in the Andes highlands.

Chili was an important trade tool long before the arrival of Europeans. Aztec rulers in South America received chilis as precious gifts, and chilis were very likely used as currency. Chili was an important food for the Aztecs as well as Mayas and Incas, and the brother of the Incas' first ruler was named Agar Uchu; *uchu* means chili.

Since long ago, chili has been, along with corn, tobacco and

◄ *Chile illustration from Leonhart Fuchs's New Kreüterbuch from 1543*

The most beautiful chili varieties:

1. Black Scorpion Tongue (picture at left)
2. Bolivian Rainbow
3. Yaki Blue Fawn
4. Fish Pepper
5. Omnicolor

chocolate, one of South America's most prized agricultural products. On the other side of the globe, in the mountainous regions of the Himalayas, chili smoke is used to clean the air and chase off bad spirits. There too, chili has been used as currency, namely along the Silk Road, the historical trading route between China, the Black Sea, and the Mediterranean.

Chilis spread, probably thanks to both humans and birds, throughout South and Central America and found their way to North America and Asia. Some species went feral along the way and can now be found in places such as Hawaii, the Solomon Islands, and the New Hebrides. These wild-growing chilis might have been the reason

earlier researchers assumed that there is wild chili from Japan and Asia. Today, however, everybody agrees that the origin of chili is in South America.

SWEDISH CHILE IN THE MIDDLE AGES

The oldest Swedish chili find is from Lund (a town in the southern Swedish province of Skåne), where they found two dried-up chili fruits from the 13th century at the site of Saint Botulf's monastery. This is 300 years earlier than if the chili had arrived with the Spanish conquistadors. Hakon Hjelmquist, professor of botany and senior lecturer at the university of Lund, wrote about the find in the Swedish book *Svensk botanisk tidskrift* in 1995. He described the fruits as small and egg-to-oval-shaped. Broken off from the hypanthium (flower cup) they measure only a scant ¼" (½ cm.) in length, and after careful examination, the professor's opinion is that they belong to Tabasco peppers, *C. frutescens* or possibly berry peppers, *C. baccatum.*

Figs and dates were found in the same hole as the peppers, which made Hjelmquist think that the chilies might have arrived in Sweden via Palestine, where, at the same time, there were famous date groves, and that the monks had brought back the chilies to use as a medicinal herb. The size and appearance of the Swedish finds correspond to the descriptions of the very first chilies found in South America. Europeans were already trading with Asia at the time, and perhaps it was in this way that the first chilis found their way to Sweden. No proof has been found to show that there was chili cultivation in Sweden at that time.

Other evidence that chili existed in Europe before the 16th century comes from the Greek philosopher and naturalist Theofrastos, who in 220 BC wrote about two different types of pepper, one of them believed to be chili. A Roman poet who lived around the year 100 wrote about a window plant with multicolored decorative leaves and fresh pepper fruits. An Arabic medical tome from 1023 mentions a plant that is probably a chili. However, there is no mention of chili in medieval European medical literature. Hjelmquist has a theory, though, that what is mentioned there as Calcutta pepper and came from India was in fact chili.

The chili fruit appeared in various parts of the world long before Columbus arrived in South America.

ARRIVAL OF THE SPANIARDS

Columbus believed he was in India when he arrived in South America in 1492. He had been sent to find the nearest sea route to Asia because the Ottoman Empire made overland travels to the East problematic. Black pepper had become a luxury item reserved for the affluent, and one goal was to find a simpler way to ensure a supply of this hot spice. When he went ashore on what is now The Dominican Republic, Columbus found a small hot fruit called *aji* (pronounced "achi") that he offered on his return to Europe. That he mistakenly called it pepper is a mistake that lives in its name even today, even though chilis and peppers have nothing in common, botanically speaking. This is what Columbus wrote in his log: "There is plenty of 'aji', which is their pepper, more precious than black pepper, and the people eat nothing else, and it is very healthy."

Columbus's discovery would have great impact on people's diets over large parts of the world. The Portuguese, who were nipping at Columbus's heels, took the chili from Brazil via Lisbon to Asia. They had established large chili plantations in Indian Goa only 30 years after Columbus's first journey, and from there the fruits spread to Thailand, Japan, China, Tibet and other countries of the region.

The chili also went to West and North Africa, as well as on to the Middle East, Italy, the Balkans, and Eastern Europe. One reason it spread so quickly was that the chili could be grown wherever the weather was warm enough. It was easily cultivated in these places and so was an economical spice, unlike the exclusive and difficult-to-grow pepper. The quick spread and popularity of chili were probably due to the fact that many were familiar with the flavor of hot pepper, and chili was reminiscent enough of pepper to replace it in existing dishes. It was a novelty while seeming familiar, unlike tomatoes and potatoes, which took much longer to become established on the other side of the Atlantic.

Linné didn't mention chili as in ingredient in food when he saw chili cultivation in Skåne, but he was upset at the practice of spicing aquavit with chili. He saw this as a kind of con trick. This is what he wrote: "Capsicum grows big and lush here and ripens under open skies. This Spanish pepper was bought by people who added it to weak aquavit to make it seem sharper and stronger, which is, in a way, a fraud."

Per Kalm, a Finnish natural historian and student of Linné, encountered chili when he visited Philadelphia, Pennsylvania, and noted that *Capsicum annum* was grown in the gardens. He described the fruit as something to be roasted along with meat or pickled like cucumbers, and sometimes mixed into a sauce. Carl von Linné officially used the names *Capsicum annuum* and *Capsicum frutescens* in the first part of his groundbreaking work *Species plantarum,* in which he described all the

Growing heirloom Espelette pepper is a cultural tradition in the southern French town of Espelette. During harvesttime, drying pepper garlands decorate many doorways and house fronts.

No one really knows how many types of chilis there are, but a guesstimate is about 3,000.

plant species known to him, and for the first time used the binomial system to name them, which quickly spread across the world. He meant that one type was annual (*annuum*) while the other was a perennial—returning—bush (*frutescens*). In 1767 Linné added the species *C. baccatum* and *C. grossum*; the latter was later assimilated with other species.

THE DIFFERENCE BETWEEN CHILI AND CHILE

The scientific name *Capsicum* is Latin for pod, or box. It appears in the writings by the Byzantine physician Actuarius of Constantinople in the 13th century. He used the Greek spelling *kapsikon*, but it is uncertain if it is only capsicum he's referring to. The first European description of *Capsicum* that we know for sure is about the chili was written by the Frenchman Joseph Pitton de Tournefort in 1719.

The word "chile" originates from the Nahuatl language of the Aztecs and other indigenous populations of South America. Their word *chilli* (pronounced chil) means "where the world ends." When the Spaniards arrived, the indigenous population called themselves "chillis men." The Spanish and Portuguese translated the word chilli into chile (pronounced tschi:le) when they brought the chili plant back to Europe. The Portuguese, who in the 16th century were competing with the Spanish for discoveries on the continent, were probably the first to call chili Spanish pepper. Once chili spread worldwide, its heat was compared to that of pepper, and in many languages chili is called pepper locally, like *piri-piri* in Swahili. Even the name paprika has its origin in the word pepper.

Chile, the country, stretches along the western coast of South America, and we can say that it has the elongated form of a cayenne pepper. Chile was part of the Incan empire and was inhabited by various indigenous peoples. Its capital, Santiago, was founded in 1541 by the Spanish and by conquistador Pedro de Valdivia. The country remained a Spanish colony until 1810, but it wasn't until 1818 that it became an independent state. They still call chili an *aji,* a word included in many chili names.

In English we refer to *chile/chili peppers* or *hot peppers*—which translates into strong paprikas, in contrast to *sweet peppers,* bell peppers. Chile is often written with an i in England, though opinions are still divided as to the correct spelling. Some say that we should spell chili with an e at the end, or cut out the word pepper that follows it. Chili pepper is the botanically correct name for *Capsicum annuum*—the Chili Pepper Group–according to the Swedish database for cultivated plants (Svensk Kulturväxtdatabas). We call them chilies in everyday parlance.

Things started to move for the chili at the end of 1980, and when chef Jonas Borssén's cookbook *Eat the Heat* was released in 1996, he quickly attracted a large following who wanted to eat hot, spicy food. Simultaneously, the import of chilies increased, and in the years following the new millenium different associations and chili groups started up, both in the physical world and online. This is a growing circle of chili enthusiasts who share their growing tips and spiciest recipes. The members range from hobby growers who seek growing tips, to extreme chili nerds who try out different growing methods, compete in eating the hottest chilies, or test every dish and chili-containing products they can find. Some even plan their holidays around visits to the most exciting chili areas.

The Swedes' interest in chili continues to rise. Proof that we're starting to "arrive" in the "chili world" is that in 2014, Sakura Holmquist from Admunstorp in Skåne received a prize in the international competition The Hot Pepper Awards, which honors the world's best chili sauces. Her sauce, Scorpion Inferno, with elements of sea buckthorn, took second place in the Scorpion category.

If you look for chili products at the grocery store, apart from sauces you'll find chili-flavored ice cream, jelly beans that both look and taste hot like chili, chili-spiced fries, and fiery hot candy. There's even tuna sauce spiced with chili, chili-cured bacon, cheese infused with chili, etc. As if that weren't enough, several new microbreweries have chili-flavored beers on tap. If you want another type of alcoholic drink, you can get an alcoholic "cooler" made from apple juice, mandarin orange, and chili; if

* https://www.chilipeppermadness.com/frequently-asked-questions/how-do-you-spell-chili-pepper-is-it-chili-chilli-or-chile/

Habanero Lemon

FRAGRANT CHILIS:

1. CAP 220 (lemon)
2. Habanero Lemon (lemon)
3. Hot lemon (lemon)
4. Habanero Naranja Picante (orange)
5. Roccoto (fragrant leaves)

you prefer to go alcohol-free, you can enjoy a beverage made from lime, chili, and ginger.

Chili hasn't just conquered the world, it has made it all the way into Swedish food culture.

CHILE IN POPULAR CULTURE

Unlike any other vegetable, chili has managed to become a pop-cultural phenomenon. It seems to be everybody's wish, from culture vultures to purely commercial brands, to be associated with chili. Research by Nadia Byrnes and John Hayes at Penn State shows that adventurous people often enjoy spicy food. Maybe it's as simple as taking a name associated with chili to come across as cool and adventurous?

The Red Hot Chili Peppers, the rock group from Los Angeles, with their characteristic style that mixes funk and hard rock, is well known in the music world, Germany has a country group called Chili, the American south has The Chili Dawgs, and in 1994 the Swedish girl trio Cayenne participated in the Eurovision Song Contest.

In Laura Esquivel's book *Like Water For Chocolate*, a young woman expresses her love and longing through her spicy cooking. The book was made into a movie in the 1990s. If you dig even deeper into the archives, you'll find the teenage movie *Hot Chili* from 1985, and the Indian thriller *Red Chilis* from 2009. The movie company Chilli Pepper Films is based in Malaysia, and the singer Rozonda Thomasi in TLC adopted

The worst names:

1. JAFSH (just another f-ing superhot)
2. Mojo Scoundrel (scoundrel = a rogue)
3. Piment de la Puta la Madre (approx. The whore mother's chili)
4. Satan's Kiss
5. Peter Pepper (alludes to penis)

the nickname Chilli. *Chili* is a comic book from Marvel Comics Group, and the heroine Chili Storm is identified by her red hair. If you like card games, there's even a game called Cayenne.

The El Paso Bicycle Club in Texas arranges a yearly bicycle race called the Chili Pepper Challenge.

THE HOTTEST PLACES IN THE WORLD

Every Fourth of July, Chili, a town in Monroe County in New York state, holds the Chil-E Festival, which draws a crowd of thousands. Each September the Pueblo Chili Festival is held in the Colorado town of Pueblo. This is a three-day-long harvest festival during which the fragrance of smoked chili enfolds the town. Espelette, a town in the French Basque country, holds a similar yearly festival during the last weekend in October—La Fête du Piment à Espelette—and is probably the only chili in the world with its own website. If you want to visit other places with chili connections, go to the small place in Illinois called Chili. Cayenne is the name of the capital in French Guyana, which is situated at the mouth of the Cayenne River on the Atlantic coast. Chiliabomwe is a town in central Zambia. Whatever you do, don't miss the state of Tabasco in southeastern Mexico, or Chile, the country, in southwestern South America.

CHILI ON EVERYTHING, AND THEN SOME

There are lots of chili gadgets out there to make your life a bit redder and more fun if it's not enough to eat, grow, and listen to chili. How about going out to the greenhouse dressed with chili-patterned garden clogs on your feet, or drink your morning coffee out of a chili-decorated coffee mug, wear chili earrings, raise a chili flag in the garden—or why not get a chili pepper tattoo?

Andy Warhol is one artist who used chilis in his artwork. Kerstin Rosengren, a textile artist, creates among other things decorative chili flowers out of wool yarn. If you wish, you can buy a suit to dress up as a chili for a party, and online you can find an alternative wedding cake topper: two plastic red chili figurines, complete with top hat and bridal veil. The only safe bet is that there is no end to chili nerds' imaginations. Why

Knitted and felted wool chili flowers, created by Kerstin Rosengren

not bend a gingerbread mold into the shape of a chili and add chili to the cookie dough? If the sky is the limit, there is the Porsche Cayenne Turbo.

CHILE IN WAR AND PEACE

In South Carolina, extremely hot chilis are grown for use in the manufacture of teargas and pepper spray. This means that the superhot element in the military's and police's pepper spray isn't pepper but chili. The heat level in pepper spray is between 2 and 5 million Scoville units. However, the use of chili against one's enemies is not some newfangled phenomenon. The Aztecs used to keep their enemies tied above chili smoke to punish them (they used a similar method to discipline their teenage sons). Chili smoke was used in the same manner before biological warfare turned into chemical combat. Chili can also work against large animals. According to *National Geographic,* farmers in certain regions of Africa burn dried chili to stave off elephants that would otherwise trample cultivations and villages. However, war can also devastate chili plantations. This has happened in Syria, where the export of chili has ceased, resulting in a lack of Aleppo chili powder worldwide. The powder is extracted from the chili of the same name, which in its fresh state is called Halabe and is much loved for its delicious aroma.

Chili is used by many boat-owners as an alternative to poisonous antifouling paint. A few spice containers of cayenne pepper mixed with 2½ quarts (2½ liters) of bottom paint is recommended as a suitable mix. Some boat-owners are experimenting with even stronger chili varieties like Carolina Reaper as an antifouling agent.

HEAT

THE WORLD'S HOTTEST VEGETABLE

$C_{18}H_{27}NO_3$

Capsaicin is an alkaloid that produces sensations of heat and pain in mammals. It is colorless and odorless, and protects the plant against pests and plant diseases like fungi. There are different alkaloids, which is why there are flavor variations among different species of chili.

CHILIS CONTAIN CAPSAICIN (can also be spelled with a k), a compound that adds a sensation of heat when eaten. The capsaicin binds to a receptor called TRPV1, which sends on information to the brain that the temperature is at least 109.4°F (43°C), which in turn provides a sensation of heat in the body. At the same time the capsaicin generates a feeling of pain, which varies depending on the amount of capsaicin in the fruit. The chemical makeup makes capsaicin a fat, which is not water soluble, which in turn explains why it is impossible to cool the heat by drinking water.

Chilis are prized by birds, which have no capsaicin receptors. They don't feel the heat and so can happily nosh on chils and spread the seeds through their excrement—a smart way for the plant to ensure its propagation. Mammals eating chili risk crushing the seeds with their teeth, so it's to the plant's advantage that various mammals think chilis taste bad (the chili couldn't know that humans were going to appreciate capsaicin).

The capsaicin compound separates chilis from all other fruits and vegetables. Of course, there are other raw foods that taste spicy, but not in quite the same way since they lack this active compound. The chili fruit's heat strength is measured in Scovilles, a measurement created especially for this purpose.

The world's hottest chili—the Carolina Reaper—has long been number 1 in the Guinness Book of Records. Which one will surpass it?

SCORCHING CULTIVATION

Ed Currie, aka Smokin' Ed, has brought out the Carolina Reaper and a line of other spicy varieties through cross-pollination. He cultivates on his farm in South Carolina, where the climate is humid and subtropical, an excellent combination for growing chilis in garden beds. Puckerbutt Pepper Company is located in the small community of Fort Mills. On his farm, Ed works in collaboration with Christopher Phillips, who collects rare chilis, growing 540 different varieties on approximately 222 acres (90 hectares).

The typical aroma of chili is so dense over the fields that it's noticeable even indoors. In a barn, newly harvested chilis are stored in big black plastic containers while waiting to be made into powder or sauce. We're talking a lot of pounds of heat! The chili handlers, who wear protective clothing with gloves and breathing masks to be able to stay in the building, must still walk outside for fresh air now and then. That's how saturated the air is with capsaicin.

Ed munches on chilis like snacks, but admits that he still feels some heat after the world record holder Carolina Reaper. To him, the taste is like a roasted sweetness, delivered with immediate heat that increases like a tidal wave until it makes you feel like your whole body is burning, producing teary eyes, profuse sweating and flailing arms. The next day, when the chili is eliminated, the butt puckers from the heat, which explains the name Pucker Butt.

Ed's goal in producing strong chili varieties is driven by his conviction that one day chili will cure cancer and reduce the risk of cardiovascular disease. With this in mind, he donates each year a large part of his harvest to the research department at the University of North Carolina at Chapel Hill.

The meeting between two "chili heads" such as Kerstin and Ed turns into a discussion about varieties, flavors, growing methods, and heat strength. It is also about how to limit your culture. Why stop at 300 or 540 varieties when there are so many more to discover? Kerstin returns to Skåne with (among others) a specimen of Chocolate Bhutlah, which, according to Ed, will be his hottest chili to date.

At the 2017 Chelsea Flower Show in London, Mike Smith, a fruit cultivator from Wales, presented an even hotter chili variety. Dragon's

Kerstin Berggren meets Ed Currie.

Breath, as Mike calls it, has registered an average of 2.48 million Scoville units. The origin of this chili is a plant called Infinity, which belongs to *the Capsicum chinense,* which has measured 1,067,286 Scoville units. An Infinity plant has been grown under strictly controlled conditions as to watering, heat, humidity, nutrients and light, and the fruits are small, similar in size to gooseberries. Mike Smith, just like Ed Currie, hopes that his chili can be useful medicinally—in Mike's case, as an anesthesia alternative for people allergic to such medications.

Dragon's Breath still has to be acknowledged as the world's hottest chili by the Guinness World Records, and according to Mike, there are no plants or seeds for sale—yet.

BREEDING PROGRAMS IN OTHER PLACES

The chili fruit is New Mexico's designated "state vegetable" and it is said that the most common question here is "Red or Green?" Chili was grown here long before it became popular in Europe. As early as in the 19th century, Fabian Garcia at New Mexico State University set about producing new varieties of chilis. New Mexico #9 arrived in 1913, and it's a variety that, in principle, changed American chili growing method and usage and cleared the way for the chili's enormous popularity in the country. It's a mild chili with a flavor reminiscent of fresh onions, a bit sweet and crisp with a hint of smokiness. When it ripens to red, you can also sense some earthiness and more heat. It replaced the traditional Mexican varieties, and what secured its success was primarily its capacity to yield large harvests, which is necessary for agricultural profitability.

Garcia's milder chili varieties made it possible to develop new areas of usage for chili. This helped the use of chili to spread to all corners of the USA, instead of keeping it a regional harvest primarily grown and consumed by the Spanish-descendant population in the southern states. The chili breeding program continued, with, among others, Paul Bosland, who founded chili's own research department at New Mexico State University in 1992: The Chile Pepper Institute. Among other things, he has developed mild varieties of jalapeños and habaneros, and lines of decorative varieties, most of which include NuMex as part of their names.

Many professional chili growers emphasize the importance of the growing location for the product's terroir (area-distinctive) taste. Chili, much like wine, gets its distinctive flavor depending on where it is grown; one important factor is the area's rock formation. The hobby grower can add minerals like rock flour, basalt rock flour, or Epsom salt (magnesium sulfate) to the pot's soil and in this way amend the fruit's flavor.

FROM SWEET TO SEARING

Bell peppers have a Scoville Heat Unit Scale (SHU) of 0, and the mildest chili varieties, such as the poblano, come in at 500–1000 SHU. Jalapeños are around 5,000, cayennes 30,000–50,000, and habaneros between 250,000 and 900,000 SHU. Bhut Jolokias are between 800,000 and 1,000,000 SHU. The Carolina Reaper, crowned the world's hottest chili in 2013, averages heat strength of 1,569,300 SHU, according to Winthrop University in South Carolina, which did the measuring. Guinness World Records confirmed this measurement. One of the fruits measured 2.2 million SHU!

Frigitello

Mild favorites:

1. Frigitello
2. Padrón
3. Jamaican Bell
4. Santa Fe Grande
5. Fenir

Caloro

Medium hot favorites:

1. Black Scorpion Tongue
2. Caloro
3. Purple Serrano
4. Chihuacle Negro
5. Fish Pepper

SCOVILLE

Chilis' heat is measured in scovilles, or Scoville Heat Units, shortened to SHU. The American chemist Wilbur Scoville developed the measuring scale in 1912, and the procedure started out as a taste testing to decide the strength of the pepper. The scale goes from 0 for bell peppers to 16 million for pure capsaicin. The measurement is derived by using ethanol to extract the chili's capsaicin, then diluting the extract with water until there is no longer any chili flavor. The more the capsaicin is diluted, the hotter the chili. The Scoville reading is 50,000 if you dilute the capsaicin 50,000 times.

Nowadays laboratories use a more accurate measuring tool called HPLC. The abbreviation stands for High Performance Liquid Chromatography. It entails drying the chili fruit and milling it to a powder that is then measured for capsaicin content by the instrument. The HPLC can also find the different types of capsaicinoids in the chili. The HPLC method is considerably more expensive, and far from all chilis have been tested this way.

10+++	1,400,000–2,100,000 SHU	*Carolina Reaper*
10++	1,000,000–1,400,000 SHU	*Dorset Naga*
10+	800,000–1,000,000 SHU	*Brown Douglah*
10	350,000–800,000 SHU	*Bhut Jolokia*
9	100,000–350,000 SHU	*Habanero*
8	50,000–100,000 SHU	*Tabasco*
7	30,000–50,000 SHU	*Black Scorpion Tongue*
6	15,000–30,000 SHU	*Cayenne*
5	5,000–15,000 SHU	*Jalapeño*
4	2,500–5,000 SHU	*Purple Tiger*
3	1,500–2,500 SHU	*Numex Suave Orange*
2	1,000–1,500 SHU	*Padrón*
1	100–1,000 SHU	*Frigitello*
0	Negligible SHU	*Bell pepper*

Trinidad Moruga Scorpion, at 1,463,700 SHU, and the Indian Bhut Jolokia, at 1,041,427, are earlier record holders.

How searing you experience a chili's heat doesn't just depend on its Scoville number, but also on the type of capsaicinoids in the fruit. Paul Bosland has developed a chili strength profile that he calls the Heat Profile, which takes into consideration the five different sensations you experience when you eat a chili.

1. Development. Does the heat come on suddenly, or is it prolonged over 5, 15, or 30 seconds?
2. Duration. Does the heat last for hours or just a few minutes?
3. Where in the mouth do you experience the heat: on the lips, at the front of the mouth, middle of the tongue, or is it pharangeal?
4. Sensation. Is it sharp as the prick of a needle, or does it spread out more like a brushstroke?
5. Intensity. Is the chili mild (0–2,000 SHU), medium (2,000–70,000 SHU), hot (70,000–500,000 SHU), or blisteringly hot (above 500,000 SHU)?

There is another scale that goes from 1 to 10 and is easier for many to relate to than the many zeroes of the Scoville scale. 10+ has been added lately for varieties between 800,000 and 1,000,000 SHU, 10++ for those up to 1,400,000 SHU, and 10+++ for the very hottest chili fruits (see table on page 63).

Habanero Brown

Hot favorites:
1. Habanero Brown
2. Habanero Caribbean Red
3. Habanero Yellow Bumpy
4. Rocoto Grandis
5. Criolla Sella

Naga Morich Chocolate

Searing hot favorites:
1. Naga Morich Chocolate
2. Yaki Blue Fawn
3. Trinidad Moruga Scorpion
4. Habanero Naranja Picante
5. Bhut Jolokia White

HELP FOR THE HEAT

Different types of Havana peppers

There are several tricks to alleviate the discomfort if, for instance, you've eaten a very strong chili by mistake, or if a child is reacting very strongly to a chili. Rule #1 is to never drink water or beer—these drinks dilute the capsaicin and make things worse. It's preferable to drink some cream or milk, since casein, milk's protein, breaks down the capsaicin. Yogurt, ice cream or other milk products will have the same effect. Casein will displace the capsaicin and take its place on the tongue. A piece of bread or pasta, or something sweet will also work. Sugar, honey or an overripe banana will do the trick, too. However, the most effective way to alleviate chili burn is to take a trip into outer space. Astronauts have reported to the Chile Research Institute in New Mexico that they don't taste any heat at all in space. It's not exactly clear why, but astronauts lose their sense of smell after a few days of weightlessness and begin to ask for heavily spiced food, especially with chili sauce.

Be careful when you give children chili, because their sensory perception is very sensitive. However, in Mexico and many countries where chili is part of the everyday diet, even 5-year-old children eat chilis and soon get used to them. Dogs and cats can react very strongly to the capsaicin, but mammals who scavenge for food in the garbage also seem to get used to the heat and there are reports on dogs that don't seem to react badly at all to chili heat.

Be careful when you handle chilis, and preferably use latex gloves when you clean, chop, and otherwise handle strong chili fruits. Whatever you do, DO NOT rub your eyes or touch any body parts with sensitive mucous membranes after you've handled chilis. It stings a lot. A LOT.

Most of the chili's heat is in the placental tissue, i.e. the white pith lining where the seeds are attached. A lot of the heat will disappear if you clean off this pith.

CHILI-EATING CHALLENGE

Chili eating contests have become incredibly popular. The internet may have played a big part in this, as you can watch people challenge themselves or others by eating very hot chili fruits on YouTube and other such sites. Claus Pilgaard, better known as Chili-Klaus, is one of them. He invites Danish celebrities to eat the world's hottest chilis, which produces predictable outcomes such as spitting, sweating, and near-fainting celebrities. Millions of viewers watch these episodes and are inspired to participate in chili challenges. Many film themselves eating the hottest chili they can get their hands on and then upload the step-by-step performance online for others to enjoy or be stunned by. You can even find chili eating competitions at fairs, cook-offs and other events. It usually isn't about eating one very hot chili fruit; instead people usually start with mild chilis and work themselves up to hotter and hotter varieties. The winner is whoever can tolerate the hottest chili.

A person's reactions after having eaten a very hot chili will vary, but here are a few common signs: hiccups, coughing, blocked ears, salivation—and a need to spit—stomachache, profuse sweating of the face and the rest of the body, involuntary gag reflex, runny nose and eyes, burping, and a strong burning sensation. It's also not uncommon to experience euphoria and happiness when the adrenaline kicks in. You might need to flap your arms, walk, or jump around to disperse the excess energy—and maybe also to try to escape the pain.

Is it dangerous to eat searing hot chilis? No, not if you're healthy. There are opposing views, but it usually concerns people who have allergic reactions, or who have had stomach or heart problems. If you're worried, don't do it! It could absolutely turn into something extremely unpleasant if you eat the very hottest varieties—an unpleasantness that can last for hours.

A seasoned chili eater can try much hotter chilis than a beginner, so if you are going to compete you'll go much further if you start ramping up your consumption of chilis a few weeks beforehand, and if you increase the amount and heat as the date of the competition draws nearer. The expression "fire butt" becomes a reality for anyone who has eaten searing hot chilis, especially if they have overdone the habaneros. Some say that the competition itself isn't difficult at all compared to the ordeal of going to the toilet the next day.

By removing the pith you can remove a lot of the chili's heat.

HOT FACTS

America has the most and perhaps also the most fanatical chili lovers. A family-owned grocery chain specializes in selling only chili sauce, and it has hundreds of different kinds. The American chili market has an almost innumerable amount of sauce brands, and in the 1990s chili sauce surpassed tomato ketchup in sales in the United States.

Every year, the International Chili Society chooses the best chili dishes and organizes countrywide local chili cook-offs throughout the United States. Each of the competition's categories has a winner, who is subsequently declared World Champion.

Chili is incredibly popular in the American South, and the climate allows chili to be grown year-round. Thus, many states consider the chili an important agricultural product. Jalapeño is by weight in pounds (kg) one of the real biggies, and the searing hot chilis are mostly grown in the southwestern United States. The largest amount of the world's chili is grown in China and India; they alone are responsible for more than half of the world's production.

SET UP YOUR OWN CHILE TASTE TEST

You can still set up a taste test—even if you don't care to compete or chomp on a CR (Carolina Reaper), BT (Butch T), or TMS (Trinidad Moruga Scorpion)—to test a few varieties, primarily the ones you grow yourself. Just cut off a small piece to taste; you don't have to eat the whole fruit, seeds, pith and all.

Put your chilis in a row, starting with the mildest and ending with the hottest. Rinse out your mouth with cream or milk between each kind to make it easier for you to distinguish between the flavors, as well as to blunt the heat. Write down and record which types you like best so you can continue to grow them next year.

EVA'S TASTE TEST:

Habanero Bella Forma—1 (700 SHU). As close to a bell pepper as it is possible to get; sweet but not as flavorful as a bell pepper.
NuMex Suave Red—2 (1,000 SHU). Mild but with a slight tendency toward heat.
Aji Llanero—3 (1,500 SHU). Mild chili and good flavor.
Trepadeira Werner—4 (2,500 SHU). Strong but not unpleasantly hot.
Jalapeño—5 (5,000 SHU). Feels milder than #4; very tasty and juicy with a heat that arrives afterhand.
Tennessee Teardrops—6 (15,000 SHU). Very fruity and tasty, however with still a relatively gentle heat.
Aji Fantasy—7 (30,000 SHU). Good and fruity with obvious heat and a surprising lemon flavor. Slightly runny nose.
Red Demon—8 (approx. 50,000 SHU). Hot, a bit bitter, just right for a Thai chili. Would willingly have used coconut milk and lime with this one. Lingering heat.
Habanero Brown—9 (100,000 SHU). Deliciously fruity, sweet and very subtle. Seriously hot but also tasty.
Mojo Scoundrel—10 (350,000 SHU). Strong heat with some fruitiness. The body starts to perspire and the heat is felt all the way down the throat.
Trinidad Moruga Scorpion—10++ (1,200,000 SHU) More than twice as hot as #10's Mojo Scoundrel. Starts out very tasty and then the heat arrives like a punch in the jaw. My face perspires, saliva is flowing, I catch my breath, I feel the heat in the entire mouth and down the throat, tears flow, my ears are blocked. Also experienced an adrenaline rush that makes me want to jump and shout YES—I did it!

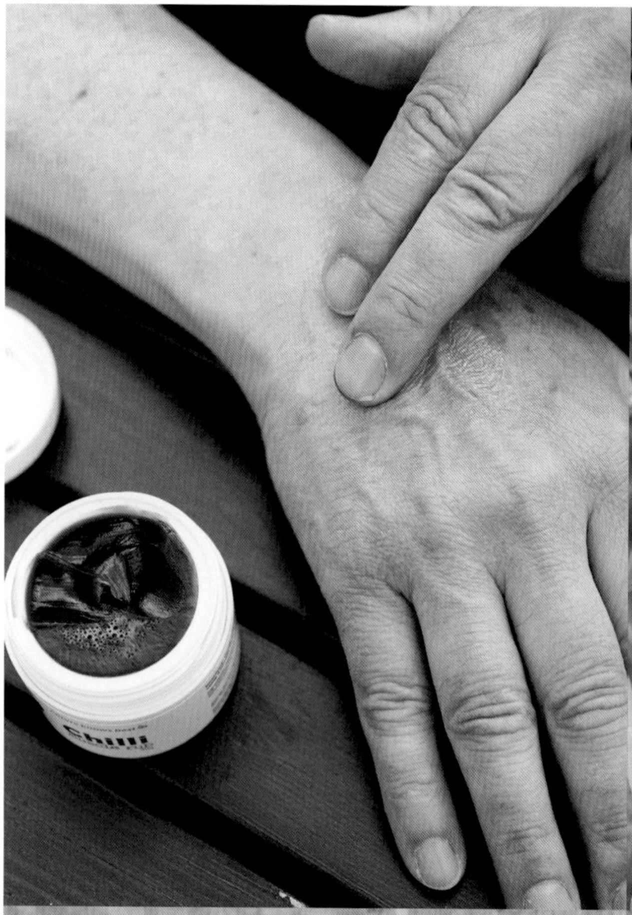
Chilli

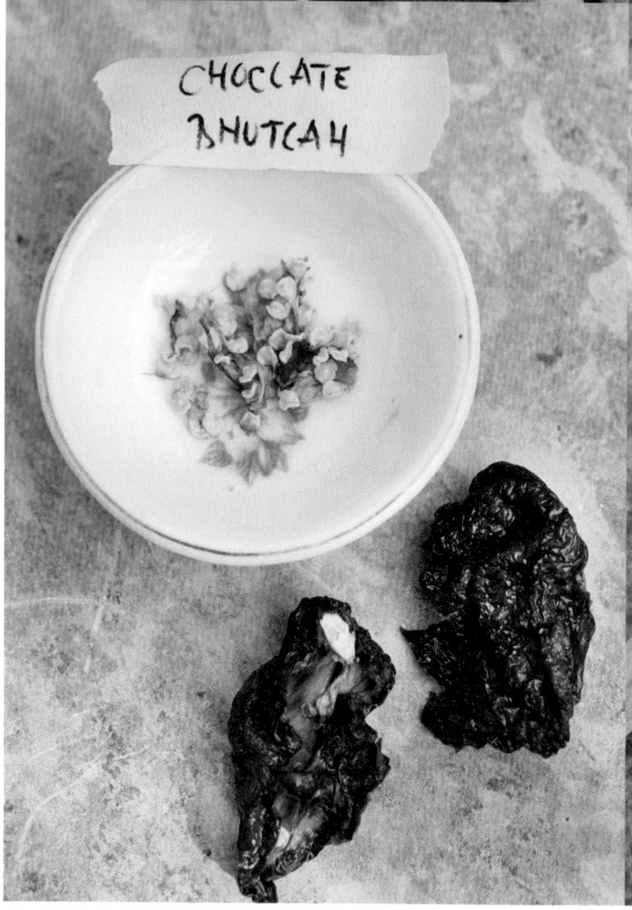
CHOCLATE
BHUTCAH

CAPSAICIN—PURE MEDICINE

Already Christopher Columbus noted that chili had been used for hundreds of years to promote good health. Research backs up that chili has a lot of health benefits. It is well documented that chili is, among other things, a pain reliever. As the capsaicin lands on the tongue and provides a burning experience, it activates the body's pain and heat receptors, which subdue pain. Chili is used to soften the pain of various ailments such as shingles, psoriasis, and fibromyalgia, but also for joint and muscle pain. When you first rub your skin with a balm or cream that contains chili, there is a burning, warm sensation that some might find uncomfortable. The pain wears off after a while. At least 6 weeks of treatment is required for lasting pain relief when dealing with more difficult pain like in cases of shingles. Food-grade oil made for food preparation (see recipe on p. 86) can be used in the same way as the creams. Remember to wash your hands carefully after each use, and do not touch your eyes.

It baffles scientists that chili works externally to alleviate pain, because they have tried to produce a more effective pain reliever than the traditional analgesic pills. These pills need to pass through the liver and intestines before the brain experiences pain relief. This takes about 20 minutes, while capsaicin works within a few seconds because the brain sends out signals as soon as the chili's heat is felt in the mouth.

Swedish research shows that sufferers of Sensory Hyper-Activity (SHR) can get relief with the help of chili. These patients suffer from nasty, hacking coughs that are often mistaken for allergies, but that cannot be alleviated by traditional asthma or allergy medications. Capsaicin tests are already used to diagnose SHR to separate these patients from those with allergies. Professor Eva Millqvist at Sahlgrenska University Hospital has discovered that her SHR patients have milder symptoms if they regularly eat food seasoned with lots of chili. By getting the body used to larger and larger amounts of heat, the olfactory sense becomes dulled. It works like a vaccine. A pilot experiment shows that patients don't have to eat the fruit itself to feel the benefit, but that capsaicin capsules work, especially to treat a hacking cough.

Maybe sometime in the future chili will be used to prevent or cure cancer, even though there is no such treatment yet. German scientists set up a study of breast cancer cells, and saw that by adding capsaicin the cells' ability to divide and multiply was reduced. Earlier research has shown mice with shrunken brain tumors after they had been injected with a substance that closely resembled capsaicin; research on mice has even shown positive results with prostate cancer.

Those suffering from stomach and intestinal troubles can get relief by consuming chili. Milder symptoms such as gas, cramps and digestive issues, for instance, are helped by increased salivation, which makes it easier for the body to break down food.

Substances in chili even promote cell renewal, so chili has a healing effect on the stomach and intestinal lining and can be used to treat stomach ulcers. Chili is an anti-inflammatory that alleviates symptoms caused by inflammation in the gut and digestive tract.

The reason chili is so often found in the daily dishes of warmer countries is partly because capsaicin counteracts bacterial and fungal growth, and can also kill harmful bacteria in food.

Back in the day, the inhabitants of the town of Espelette in southern France covered fresh meat with chili powder to make it last longer and to decrease the risk of food poisoning.

Chili is rich in vitamins and minerals such as vitamin A, vitamin C, and several of the B vitamins together with magnesium, potassium, and calcium. These substances improve the body's ability to absorb nutrients from other foods, and they strengthen the immune system. This decreases your risk of catching colds, for instance, and other viruses. Chili even boosts the metabolism a little, but not enough to work as a diet aid. Red chilis contain carotene, while yellow and orange fruits contain beta-carotene. These substances are changed to vitamin A in the body, which among other things promote good eyesight and cell growth. Anyone who eats a lot of beta-carotene gets a slightly golden skin as a bonus, just as when you eat a lot of carrots.

Endorphins, the body's own morphine, are released when we eat chili, which, apart from being a pain reliever, also induces euphoria. That's why chili is slightly addictive, and those who eat lots of chili want more! This mix of delight and pain will also give you a kick of adrenaline if you eat the seriously hot chilis—a bit like bungee jumping or car racing. The endorphin rush also raises your blood pressure and dilates the blood vessels, which is one of the reasons why you perspire when you eat chili.

Chili is both a vessel dilator and a blood thinner, which means you can eat chili to prevent cardiovascular problems. Even the smallest vessels—the capillaries—dilate to make the blood flow quicker, which improves circulation in the brain, fingers, and toes. Capillaries are also in the sex organs, which contribute to increased sexual arousal in both sexes, and improve a man's ability to achieve and keep an erection.

Perspiration caused by chilis alleviates a stuffy nose and tension headache. Chili can be used to regulate body temperature. Eat chili to raise your body temperature when in a cold climate, or to start a cooling sweat when you're overheating! Those who have trouble perspiring can get it going by eating chili.

Hillary Clinton's use of chili fruits is just one example of how chili is used as a household remedy. She ate chili fruits during her time as US Secretary of State to have the stamina for a hectic work schedule, and to counteract jet lag from her travels all over the world. Kim Ghatta, the BBC reporter who followed Clinton on her trips, said that Clinton ate chilis to perspire and to "cleanse the system."

You can reap the health benefits of chilis by eating fresh or dried chilis often—preferably every day. If you want to use chili as a cure, like reducing the risk of catching a cold, make a tea with fresh or dried chili, as hot as possible. Let about ⅕ oz. (5 g.) of chili steep in hot water for 5 minutes (let it steep for 10 minutes if you use dried chili) and then drink this 2–3 times a day for a week. You can even take chili in capsules.

ANCHO

TASTE

HARVEST AND RECIPES

YOU SOW, WATER, fertilize, putter around, fight pests and cold winds, and then, one day, finally, the plants are covered in the most beautiful, tastiest and most wonderful fruits you can imagine. You are in chili heaven!

There are so many different chili dishes that you can make a new one every day of the year without putting a dent in your activity of tasting the world's hot dishes. In all South American countries, in Mexico, in large parts of North America and Asia, in the Middle East, and in most of the African countries, chili is part of the everyday diet. Even in Europe chile is a part of many dishes, like in the cuisines of Hungary, Spain, and Italy.

South America is the chili's homeland, and the South Americans have really taken this vegetable to heart. Aji is a traditional Chilean sauce from tomatoes, onions, fresh cilantro, lemon, some oil, and—chili. The chili is often the medium hot Cacho de Cabra or Goat Weed. Ceviche, a fish concoction, is almost Peru's national dish. Bolivians love their Pique a lo Macho, a type of meat salad replete with large pieces of Locoto chili (Rocoto). The one who can eat the entire dish is considered real "macho"—the name of the dish means to "wake a macho"—and in Brazil people willingly tuck into chicken dishes containing the popular Malagueta chili.

Can anyone imagine Mexico without tacos, enchiladas, and mole sauce? Dried or smoked chilis like chipotle and ancho are also popular there. They're often soaked and mashed with a mortar and pestle, and then added to stews and sauces. The West Indies is another stage for chilis. It is primarily the hot and fruity habanero that is used in the Caribbean world, often together with sweet and exotic fruits. Combine the chili with coconut and you're guaranteed Caribbean flavor! The popular Jamaican jerk spice mix wouldn't be jerk if it didn't include chili.

The American south has adopted the fiery food culture, which is obvious in Louisiana's Cajun cooking. The borders of Mexico have given us chili con carne, and the popular jalapeño popper snacks that are often served at halftime during football or basketball games in the South.

Asian cuisine has always been heavily spiced, and chili quickly became natural when it was introduced in the 16th and 17th centuries. It's difficult to imagine Indian curry dishes and tandoori without the chili. Bhut Jolokia comes from northern India, where we find especially searing dishes. Thai cooking would of course not be Thai without the chili—soup like *tom yum* made with chicken or shrimp is just one example. Pad Thai, a noodle dish, and the papaya salad called *som tam* are two more. A long line of Vietnamese and Filipino dishes, as well as the Indonesian Nasi Goreng, would hardly exist if it weren't for the chili fruit. A Korean meal without kimchi would definitely be lacking something! Sichuan and Hunan are Chinese provinces known for their fiery food. Here the red chili symbolizes the Chinese communist revolution. Mao Zedong allegedly said, "The food of the true revolutionary is the red pepper, and he who cannot endure red peppers is also unable to fight." The chili paste Ciba lajiao, made with dried chili soaked overnight and then mixed with ginger and garlic, is an important ingredient in stews and soups called *huo guo*, which means fiery stew.

The chili conquered Africa in a similar way, and chili now has its rightful place in much of the continent's food culture. Americans brought the chili to North Africa, and harissa, a hot sauce, is very popular. Europeans introduced the chili to West Africa, and chili sauce is eaten with almost everything, even at breakfast. It is said that every family has their own hot sauce recipe.

Peanuts and chilis are often combined in Central African dishes, and you'll find an Indian influence in the food culture of both South Africa and Malawi. This means that hot dishes like samosas are very popular. Nali, also called "Africa's hottest sauce" is made from the Malawi Birdseye chili, and the sauce is an important ingredient in the country's cooking.

Middle Eastern food can also be spicy, but it is primarily very flavorful, often with deep notes of mild chili powders. Falafel with chopped chili is super tasty; try to mix in a grilled and peeled chili fruit into hummus next time, or sprinkle it with some finely ground chili powder before serving for a delicious kick! Many stews in Syria, Lebanon and Palestine are seasoned with chili or harissa.

Most European cuisine has always been more careful in its use of chili. However, in Hungary, chili and paprika pepper are seen as national spices and goulash is the national dish. The Spanish eat a lot of chili. A very popular tapas dish, Piementos de Padrón, is made with grilled green Padrón chilis, olive oil, and salt. From Spain and Portugal we also get chorizo, a very spicy dry sausage. Gazpacho and Mojo Rojo sauce are two other Spanish classics. Dried Piment d'Espelette, from the Basque border region between France and Spain, is a staple in that regional cuisine.

Spaghetti aglio, spaghetti with garlic and chili, is a very popular everyday dish in Italy. Mild, small, round chilis—pepperoncini—stuffed with a cheese or tuna filling and packed in oil are also much enjoyed.

Maybe it is because British people have learned to love spices that Indian food has been elected the most popular cuisine in Britain. Chicken tikka is a long-standing favorite, but its status is threatened by jalfrezi, an even more fiery dish.

Swedes, just like the Brits, like to eat other countries' food, and often dishes containing chili. The Swedish daily diet is hardly known for its spiciness, but it is of course more than possible to use chili to turn up the heat and flavor a notch on traditional everyday dishes. How about adding some chili to meatballs or Jansson's Temptation? There are no food taboos among chili nerds! Chili is such a multi-faceted fruit that you can eat it with just about everything.

AN EXCESS OF CHILE

You'll soon realize, even in your utter euphoria over a large chili harvest, that there is no way that you and your family will be able to eat all that fresh chili, and that you'll have to do something to preserve the chili as long as possible—at least until it is time for next year's harvest.

Here are some suggestions:

- Freeze
- Dehydrate
- Smoke
- Salt
- Make sauce
- Make oil/vinegar
- Pickle them
- Make candy

HEADS UP! Always sterilize the jars you are using for pickles, preserves, sauces, and similar food items. Wash the jars and lids, then place them in boiling water for a few minutes, and then dry them in the oven at 212°F (100°C). It is important to practice good food hygiene by washing hands and using clean utensils to avoid harmful bacteria. Rinse off all grit and dirt thoroughly that are on the vegetables you are using. If you're repurposing old jars, rub some food-grade oil on the old labels to make them easier to remove.

Dry goods like chili powder should be stored at room temperature in a dry, dark environment. This goes for vinegar and oil, too. Sauces, pickles, and preserves should always be kept refrigerated. Remember to use latex gloves when you handle chilis, and especially when you cut them to remove the seeds and pith. Keep out of the vapors when you blend or boil chilis.

CHILIS IN THE REFRIGERATOR AND FREEZER

Chilis soon start to wither and dry up when kept at room temperature. If you want to preserve their juiciness and freshness, you'll have to keep them in a plastic bag in the refrigerator—preferably with a damp paper towel or two. To store them even longer, chop them finely and freeze them. Small plastic resealable bags (the smallest size can be found in office supply stores) work fine. It's easy to take just the right amount for different dishes, and the taste is as close to fresh as you can get.

HOW TO DEHYDRATE CHILE

The most common and also the best way to preserve chilis is to dehydrate them. They can be dried at room temperature, or more quickly in the oven or in a dehydrator. Remember, though, to remove the seeds if needed for future use, as too high a temperature will make the seeds nonviable.

Hanging the chili to dry at room temperature works well if the room is dry and warm. However, thick-skinned varieties can, at worst, become moldy. Push the pin through the stem and not the fruit if you're going to hang the chili. Otherwise the risk is high that the fruit will be infected mold fungus. Take down the fruits as soon as they are dry or

FRESH—DRIED CHILE

Marisol	➤	Guajillo
Jalapeño	➤	Chipotle or Morita
Poblano	➤	Ancho or Mulato
Chilac	➤	Pasilla
Bola	➤	Cascabel Rattlesnake
Anaheim	➤	Seco del Norte California chili pod Chili de la Tierra
Serrano	➤	Seco

they'll get too dusty, their color will be bleached out, and their flavor will deteriorate.

The shorter the drying time, the more taste the chili will keep, and the quickest way to dehydrate a chili is to use the oven—preferably on a convection setting—or a dehydrator.

It's best to dry the chilis at a temperature of 104°F–122°F (40°C–50°C) because many nutrients are destroyed when the temperature exceeds 122°F (50°C). That way the flavor remains intact, as the drying time is relatively short. The chili can taste burned if it is dried at too high a temperature. It's up to you if you want to dry the chilis with or without the seeds and pith. Large or thick-skinned chilis should be halved or cut into wedges to dry out quicker.

Dried fruits are kept in dark jars or in a cupboard, because daylight negatively affects both flavor and color. You can mix the dried fruit into flakes or grind them to a powder. The fruits need to be dry as dust before you mix them in a mixer or electric coffee grinder.

HOW TO SMOKE CHILE

It's a Mexican tradition to smoke and dry chilis, and there the chili changes name when it is smoked, dried or both. For example, smoked green (unripe) jalapeño becomes chipotle, and smoked red (ripe) jalapeño is called Morita. Chile Bola becomes Casabel when dried, and also Rattle Chile because when the seeds loosen inside the fruit it sounds like a rattle.

Red (ripe) poblano is called ancho when dried, while the one that turns brown when ripe is called Mulato when sun-dried. Fresh Chilaca changes its name to Pasilla when dried, and Marisol becomes guajillo. These chilis are used for salsas as well as cooked dishes, and they are often crushed with a mortar and pestle before use. In Mexico, ancho, Mulato, and Pasilla are mentioned as "the holy trinity of chilis." These days it is popular to smoke many different types of chilis, but they don't change names like the traditional chilis.

The chili retains its fruity flavor when cold smoked at temperatures between 59°F (15°C) and 86°F (30°C). The easiest way to do this is to use a smoker box or a smoking gun, or—the simplest way—your round,

The spiral-shaped insert is filled with finely milled chippings, then placed in the grill and lit. Don't forget to put on the lid!

covered grill with an insert for smoking. Use fine-milled chippings, like sawdust, which you set in the spiral-shaped insert at the bottom of the grill, and then light with a strong flame. Fresh or semi-dried (half dried) chilis are placed on a platter on top of the grill's grate. Put on the lid, leaving a narrow opening for air circulation. The chippings burn slowly for about 10 hours and develop smoke that flavors the chili. The chili is dried in a dehydrator or an oven after smoking until it is completely dried out. It can now be stored in a glass jar until it will be used.

You can also hot smoke chili, but the temperature should not exceed 158°F (70°C).

CHILI
BBQ
CHILI SALT

HOMEMADE SPICE MIX

Vary your dried and ground chili powder by mixing your own spice mixes. For example, make your own grill spice or BBQ rub, or make garam masala. Oregano, cumin, and mustard seeds make good friends for the chili powder.

BBQ RUB
1 tbsp chipotle or ancho powder
1 tbsp salt flakes
½ tbsp dried oregano
½ tbsp coarsely ground black pepper
½ tbsp coriander seed
½ tbsp crushed yellow mustard seeds
1 tsp dried rosemary
1 tbsp brown sugar
½ tsp licorice powder, instant coffee powder, or cumin—optional

Mix all the ingredients together. Store in a glass jar away from light until ready to use. This can be used instead of traditional grill spice or as a BBQ rub, i.e., a dry marinade for meat before grilling.

GARAM MASALA
1 tbsp turmeric
1 tbsp black pepper, freshly ground
1 tsp nutmeg
1 tbsp cinnamon
½ tbsp cumin
½ tbsp cloves
1 tbsp salt
1 tsp chili powder
½ tsp cardamom

Mix the spices and use immediately, or store in a dark jar.

CHILE SALT
The easiest way to make chili salt is to mix chili powder with the desired amount of salt. Even better is to mix fresh chili with coarse salt, as the salt absorbs the chili juices and preserves both the heat and flavor much better. Spread the newly mixed salt on a tray to dry. You choose the proportions you like—the more chili you use and the hotter it is, the more intense the salt. 6¾ fl. oz. (2 dl.) coarse salt is a good benchmark to work with. You can mix the chili salt once more once it has dried to prevent it from becoming hard and caked.

CHILE OIL

Mixing chili and oil is more iffy than chili and vinegar, because bacteria can develop in the oil and make the oil unpalatable. In the worst-case scenario, poisonous botulism bacteria can develop, which could be life-threatening. It is extremely important to use good hygiene if you mix fresh chili and oil, and to use the chili oil the next day at the latest, or freeze it in an ice cube tray. The poison is killed by heat, so if you want to make a longer-lasting oil, heat the oil together with the chili—dried chili is good. Heat the mixture to at least 176°F (80°C) for 10 minutes to kill any poisonous spores.

Peruvian chile oil

PERUVIAN CHILE OIL

$3^{1}/_{3}$ fl. oz. (1 dl.) Aji Amarillo

$3^{1}/_{3}$ fl. oz. unflavored oil

Mix the fruit, pour the oil over, mix to a fine consistency, and mix again. Unheated chili oil has very short shelf life. Store in the refrigerator or freeze.

HOT CHILE OIL

6¾ fl. oz. (2 dl.) peanut oil

4 dried chili fruits, such as Habanero Lemon or Scotch Bonnet

Halve the fruits. Heat the oil without bringing it to a boil, and add in the chilis. Let them steep for 10–15 minutes, and keep watch so the mix doesn't come to a boil. Pour everything into a thoroughly cleaned jar and let the oil sit for 2 weeks at room temperature.

Hot chile oil and chile vinegar

CHILE VINEGAR

The simplest way to make vinegar is to let fresh or dried chilis steep in apple cider or white wine vinegar. Vinegar is acidic, which makes it difficult for harmful bacteria to survive. Let the chili steep in the vinegar for about a week, and then strain the liquid. Taste test a few times while it is maturing. The shelf life is about 1 year.

Add heat to your aquavit by letting a chili fruit steep in the alcohol. Here, a piece of vanilla bean got in, too.

AQUAVIT AND ALCOHOL-FREE BEVERAGES

Do as the 18th-century Swedish inhabitants from the southern province of Skåne did—flavor aquavit with chili! You make chili aquavit more or less the same way as chili vinegar, because harmful bacteria can't grow in alcohol. Slice a chili fruit (or add a whole fruit) and let it steep in aquavit special (an aquavit suitable for cocktails, and for making flavored aquavit), vodka or other neutral alcohol, maybe along with a vanilla bean, a slice of kumquat, and aniseed or other spice of your choice. Let steep for a week or two (taste test!) and then strain of the fruits to get a shot of hot chili aquavit!

You can also crumble some dried chili into a cup of hot water or herb tea if you want to warm yourself without using alcohol. Why not get that kick by adding chili to hot apple juice and serve as an alternative to mulled cider?

Pickled chili

CHILI WITH EVERYTHING

As we've seen, almost anything can be flavored with chili if you want the heat or flavor: springtime's asparagus with chili mayonnaise, summer's fiery gooseberry jam, fall's spicy apple pie, and winter's smoking soups and stews. All the pickles and preserves you want to add an extra zing to needs chili: chutney, kimchi, beets, Boston cucumber pickles, and, of course, pickled vegetables. Why not make jars of fefferoni, or put them in a classic 1–2–3 liquid, which goes very well with meat as well as vegetarian stews? Use your regular recipes, or search Google for new ones and add chilis as desired.

PICKLED JALAPEÑOS
1½ lb–1¾ lb (700–800 g.) jalapeños—different colors look nice
2–3 cloves of garlic
1 tsp mustard seeds—optional

PICKLING LIQUID
1 cup + 1 tsp (2½ dl.) apple cider vinegar
3 cups + 1 tbsp (7½ dl.) water
2½ fl. oz. (3/4 dl.) granulated sugar
1 tsp salt

Boil the ingredients for the pickling liquid for a few minutes. Cut the chili in 1/5" (5 mm.) thick slices and put them in the liquid along with the garlic cloves and mustard seeds, if using. Let simmer, covered, for 2–3 minutes. Fish out the jalapeño slices and place them into thoroughly cleaned jars. Pour the liquid over them and cover with a lid. Store in the refrigerator.

PICKLED CHILIS
3 1/3 fl. oz. (1 dl.) distilled vinegar at 5%
6¾ fl. oz. (2 dl.) granulated sugar
1¼ cup (3 dl.) water
10–15 chili fruits

Bring the pickling liquid to a boil and let it cool. Slice the chilis in half and remove the seeds. Place the chilis in a thoroughly cleaned jar and pour the cold pickling liquid over them. Let steep in the refrigerator for at least 1 week to let the fruits develop nicely.

KIMCHI

1 head Chinese or pointy cabbage
4 tsp iodine-free salt
1 tart apple
1$^{1}/_{5}$"–1½" (3 cm.–4 cm.) fresh ginger
3 large garlic cloves
1 tbsp dried chili, preferably Gochugaru
1 fresh chili, Korean Hot for example

Take extra care with food hygiene when making Kimchi, as it might go moldy otherwise. Only use fresh, organically grown vegetables (organically grown vegetables contain natural lactid acid bacteria that will start the fermenting process. There is a high risk that the batch of kimchi might not take if you use pesticide-sprayed vegetables.)

Finely shred the cabbage, grate the rootstock, and cover with the salt. Grate the apple, ginger, and garlic. Finely chop the fresh chili fruit. Add the remaining ingredients to the shredded cabbage and knead thoroughly. The cabbage will render its liquid. Press down on it with a closed fist and pummel with a pestle if you have to. Place everything in a jar with an airtight lid, but don't fill the jar more than three fourths of the way up. Make sure that the liquid covers the cabbage, otherwise you'll need to continue to knead/pummel it into the jar. All the vegetables must be covered with liquid. To protect the kimchi from air bubbles, place a plastic bag in the jar, fill it up with water so the bag works as a lid over the kimchi. Tie up the bag and screw on the jar lid. Leave the jar at room temperature for 14 days. You can open the jar after 2 weeks and taste test the kimchi. Let ripen for a week or two in the refrigerator.

CHILI PATÉ

8–10 mild chili fruits, preferably large and meaty ones like Padrón, poblano, or Anaheim
4–5 garlic cloves
2–3 tbsp canola oil
$^{1}/_{5}$ tsp salt

Sliver the chili and garlic. Fry the mixture in the oil for about 10–15 minutes along with the salt, and then mix it into a smooth paté. Pour into thoroughly cleaned jars. It's delicious on a sandwich or cheese cracker or as a dip.

Chili Paté and *Gooseberry Jam with a Kick* (p. 93)

Black Scorpion Tongue Jelly

CHILE SWEETS

It's not for nothing that we can find chili ice cream and chili chocolate bars. Sweetness and chili make a great match. Bake your own chili cookies using what you have on hand—mild or hot chilis—depending of what flavor experience you're looking for. Make your own chocolate flavored with chili; roll toasted almonds in chili powder; bake your most delicious cookies and add chili powder; or flavor an apple pie with your favorite chili. Jams, fruit squashes, and jelly can handle a somewhat hotter chili. Let's bang the drum for apple and chili flavored fruit leather. It's so good it's almost addictive! Do you dare to put candy coating on a searing hot chili? Don't forget . . . a fruity chili sauce is especially delicious with ice cream, chocolate cake, stewed pears, or a fruit salad.

HIMLABACKEN'S CHILI COOKIES

3½ oz. (100 g.) butter
1¼ cup (3 dl.) rolled oats
scant ¼ cup (½ dl.) granulated sugar
5 fl. oz. (1½ dl.) all-purpose flour
½ tsp deer horn salt (baker's ammonia)
½ tsp chili powder; a mixture or use your own favorite
zest of one lemon
juice of ½ lemon
1 tsp sea salt

Melt the butter and mix it with the other ingredients. Shape the dough into logs and place them In plastic wrap. Let the dough sit in the refrigerator for 1 hour. Remove the plastic wrap, slice the logs into thin cookies, and place them on cookie sheets lined with parchment paper. Bake in a 350°F (175°C) for about 15 minutes. Store in an airtight cookie tin.

BLACK SCORPION TONGUE JELLY

2¼ lbs (1 kg) crabapples
6¾ fl. oz. (2 dl.) water
1½ lb (650 g.) sugar per quart drained crabapple liquid
4–6 tsp Black Scorpion Tongue flakes

Rinse the crabapples and cut them in half. Bring the apples and water to boil in a large saucepan over low heat, and cook until the apples are soft and mushy. Pour the apple mash into a fruit squash strainer and let drain for 1 hour.

Measure the crabapple liquid into a large saucepan and add 1½ lbs of sugar per quart liquid. Bring to a boil and let boil for 7–8 minutes. Skim off the froth that collects on the liquid's surface. Add the chili flakes, and pour the jelly into small jars. Place lids on the jars but don't screw them down until the jelly has cooled.

The jelly takes between 12 and 24 hours to set, depending on how ripe the crabapples are. Store the jelly in the refrigerator.

GOOSEBERRY JAM WITH A KICK

1 quart (1 liter) gooseberries
1–2 chili Omnicolor
1 lb 1¾ oz. (500 g.) sugar for jam making

Rinse and clean the gooseberries. Halve the chili fruits and remove the seeds. Put the berries and chilis in a saucepan with the sugar. Slowly bring the contents to a boil to allow the sugar to dissolve. Stir. Boil vigorously for 2–3 minutes. Pour the mixture into warm jars and let cool.

APPLE CHILI FRUIT LEATHER

4½ lbs (2 kg) apples
3⅓ fl. oz. (1 dl.) water
½ tsp chili powder

Remove the apple seeds and peel the apples. Cut them into wedges and place them in a large saucepan. Pour in the water and bring to a boil. Let simmer for 5–10 minutes or until the apples are soft. Mix to an even blend and add the chili powder.

Spread the apple mixture as evenly as possible on two cookie sheets lined with silicon mats. The mixture should be about ⅕" (4 mm.) thick. Dry the leathers in the oven at 302°F (150°C) for 6–8 hours, or until the leathers are no longer sticky. Cut the fruit leather into thin strips and roll them up into candy rolls.

A WORLD OF SAUCES

Chili sauce is worth its very own chapter. This is obvious when you step into most grocery stores, which typically have several shelves full of different chili sauces such as Tabasco, harissa, and sweet chili sauce. These are sauces that those of you who grow your own chili obviously can make yourself. If you like *sambal oelek*, Mexican mole, salsa verde, or the popular Sriracha, well, then that's the sauce you should make. Chili marries very well with the sweetness of fruit and berries, and it is common in other countries to find chili sauces that contain exotic fruits such as mango, pineapple, melon or papaya. It works just as well with berries or fruits you grow in your garden or pick in the wild, like blueberries, raspberries, sea buckthorn, or strawberries.

SHELF LIFE

A rule of thumb is that a cold-prepared sauce doesn't store well, while a sauce that has been cooked keeps longer. Fermentation, lactic acid fermentation, prolongs a cold sauce's shelf life. Salt and sugar have bacteria-killing properties, which translates to a longer shelf life. An unopened jar keeps longer than one that has been opened, and the more often you dip a spoon in the sauce, the bigger risk that the sauce will go moldy. That's why it is difficult to set any hard-and-fast rules as to how long a sauce will keep—it can vary from a few days to a year.

It matters a lot what kind of chili you use for your sauce, not just for the heat but also for the flavor. Is it going to be a chili with fruity notes, a citrus taste, or the deep flavor of a smoked chili? Taste test your chilis and analyze the flavors carefully—what is it in here more than the heat that makes you prefer this version? What would pair well with it?

FLAVORS THAT MARRY WELL WITH CHILE

- Lime
- Ginger
- Coriander
- Cumin
- Basil
- Garlic
- Onion
- Beans
- Nuts
- Tomato
- Tomatillo
- Coconut milk
- Apple cider
- Vinegar
- Peanuts

Fermented chili sauce, page 97

SRIRACHA

FERMENTED CHILI SAUCE

1 lbs 1¾ oz. (500 g.) chili fruits—all the same kind or color, or a mix of different fruits
Non-iodized sea salt
1 quart (1 liter) water
3⅓ fl. oz.–6¾ fl. oz. (1dl–2 dl.) apple cider vinegar
Glass jars, preferably with clamp-down lid with rubber seal

Halve the chili fruits and remove all the seeds. Fill the glass jars with the chilis. You'll get different sauce flavors/colors if you place each chili variety and color in separate jars. Why not make one mild and one furiously hot?

Mix sea salt, water, and vinegar until the salt has dissolved. You'll have to let the water cool before you continue the process if you've warmed it. Pour the brine over the chilis in the jar so they are covered. They have to be completely submerged—not even a seed is allowed to go above the surface. If you place a plastic bag on the surface and fill it with water you'll weigh down the chili fruits so they stay underwater. You can close the jar if you use jars with clamp-down lids and a rubber seal. If you're using another type of jar, just fasten the lid loosely—it is important that air can escape during the fermentation process, but no air is allowed to enter.

Let stand for 10 days at room temperature. Strain the salty brine in a bowl. Mix the chili fruits and add water (from the brine) a little at a time while you're mixing. Season them with apple cider vinegar until you have the desired consistency and taste. The brine contains both heat and flavor, so the more brine you add, the hotter the sauce. If you want a milder sauce, increase the amount of cider vinegar. Store the sauce in the refrigerator. It will keep for about 1 year.

SRIRACHA

In Thailand, its country of origin, Sriracha is eaten primarily with different kinds of shellfish. However, in the United States, where the sauce has become incredibly popular in the last few years, you can see it used on, among other things, pizza and spring rolls and in beer (!). The original sauce has to go through the fermentation process, but you can skip it even though the flavor won't develop fully.

1 lb 1¾ oz. (500 g.) jalapeños (ripe, red fruits)
5 garlic cloves
3 tbsp brown sugar
2 tbsp non-iodized salt
5 fl. oz. (1½ dl.) white wine vinegar

Remove the stalk, but leave the seeds and pith in the fruits. Mix them finely with garlic, sugar, and salt, and pour the mixture into a thoroughly cleaned glass jar. Cover with plastic wrap and leave the jar at room temperature. Stir the mixture every day. The sauce will start to ferment after 2 to 4 days, which is the purpose of storing it at room temperature. Continue to stir the mixture every day (if the sauce turns moldy it will be inedible, but cloudy-looking water is normal). The fermentation is done after 5 to 6 days. Pour the sauce back into the mixer and add the vinegar. Mix thoroughly and pass the mixture through a sieve so you end up with a purée without seeds or bits of peel. Cook the purée for 5–10 minutes to desired consistency. Let the sauce cool and store it in the refrigerator. The sauce will keep for about 1 year.

TABASCO
HARISSA
SWEET CHILI
AMBAL OELEK

SWEET CHILI SAUCE

3 chili fruits, golden cayenne or Malawi Birdseye for example
1 clove garlic
$3^1/_3$ fl. oz. (1 dl.) apple cider vinegar
$3^1/_3$ fl. oz. (1 dl.) water
$3^1/_3$ fl. oz. (1 dl.) sugar with pectin
$^1/_5$ tsp salt

Remove the chili seeds if you don't want them and chop the fruits. Finely chop the garlic clove. Place all the ingredients in a saucepan and bring to a boil. Let it cook 5–10 minutes. Taste and add more chili if needed, depending on how strong a sauce you want. Pour the sauce into thoroughly cleaned jars or bottles. Store in the refrigerator. The sauce will keep for about 6 months.

SAMBAL OELEK

5 red jalapeños or other medium hot chili fruits
3 Piri Piri or Thai Bird chilis
2 tsp salt
3½ fl. oz. (1 dl.) sugar
3½ fl. oz. (1 dl.) lime juice

Finely chop the chili fruits—it's okay if some seeds are left. Place the chopped fruits in a saucepan with the other ingredients. Cook for 5 minutes, taste and add more chili if you want a hotter sauce. Cook for another 2–3 minutes. Let the sauce cool and pour it into bottles. The sauce will keep for about 6 months.

HARISSA

3 large mild chili fruits, like Anaheim
1 tsp dried chili flakes
2 fresh, hot, piri piri type chili fruits
1 garlic clove
1 tsp coriander seed
1 tsp caraway seed
1 tsp cumin
¾ tsp salt

Grill the mild chili fruits in the oven at 390°F (200°C) for about 10–15 minutes. The peel should turn black. Remove the chilis from the oven and place them in a bowl with a lid or put some plastic wrap over it for a few minutes. Pull off the peel and let the chilis cool.

Remove the seeds and finely chop the other chilis, and finely chop the garlic clove. With a mortar and pestle, crush the different chili seeds together with chili flakes and garlic if you wish. Mix together all ingredients and taste test. Store in the refrigerator. The harissa will last for about 1 year.

TABASCO-LIKE SAUCE

3½ fl. oz. chili fruit, tabasco or Malawi Birdseye for example
3½ fl. oz. white wine vinegar
1½ tsp salt

Finely chop the chilis; put all the ingredients in a saucepan, and bring them to a boil. Let simmer for about 5 minutes. Mix to a smooth sauce. True Tabasco sauce ripens in oak barrels for 3 years. For a homemade version, add a few oak chips to the sauce and let the Tabasco sauce steep for at least 2 weeks in the refrigerator. Strain the sauce off the oak chips and pour it into small, slim bottles.

FRUITY SAUCE

Sweet fruits with chili heat is a classic combination. Mango is often used, but there are many Swedish fruits that work just as well. Try raspberries, sea buckthorn, gooseberries, bilberries or strawberries, for example. The hotter the chili, the "cooler" the sauce—it's just the combination of hot and sweet that makes it so absolutely delicious. This sauce is as good with savory dishes as with dessert—perhaps on ice cream or with chocolate cake?

14 oz. (400 g.) fruit
2–3 chili fruits—try habanero or Rocoto here
1¾ fl. oz.–3⅓ fl. oz. granulated sugar
1 tsp salt
scant 1¾ fl. oz. apple cider vinegar or distilled white vinegar
1 tbsp white wine vinegar—optional
1 garlic clove—optional

Halve the fruits, remove the seeds, and then chop the chili fruits. Cook them with the remaining ingredients for about 10 minutes. Sweet fruits require less sugar and more acidic liquid (vinegar), and sour fruits need more sugar. The thrill here is the combination of sweet, salt, and heat. You can, of course, make a fruity sauce with mild chilis, but that kind of misses the point. Keep testing during the preparation to make sure that the sauce tastes just as you want it to. Store the sauce in the refrigerator. It will keep for about 6 months.

HABANERO SALSA

The heat of the habanero chili is perfectly balanced by the tart tamarind paste, the onion's and tomatoes' sweetness, and the acidic lemon juice. This salsa works equally with grilled food or as a hot dip.

scant 1¾ fl. oz. (½ dl.) tamarind paste
1 or 2 lemons
3 garlic cloves
2 habanero chilis
1 jalapeño
½ red onion
2 tomatoes
a bunch of fresh onion, spring onions or chives for example
3⅓ fl. oz. (1 dl.) olive oil
salt
Garnish: lime and cilantro

Let the tamarind paste soak in 6¾ fl. oz. (2 dl.) water for 15 minutes. During this time, squeeze the lemon(s) to get 3⅓ fl. oz. (1 dl.) lemon juice. Grate the garlic cloves, finely chop the chilis, tomatoes, red onion, and fresh onions. Squeeze out the water from the tamarind paste, and throw away the paste, but keep the water. Mix all the ingredients and blend them to a smooth sauce, and season with salt. Serve the sauce in an attractive bowl and garnish with lime and cilantro. Store the salsa in the refrigerator, where it will keep for about one week.

Fruity sauces

Jalapeño poppers—some are deep-fried in batter.

JALAPEÑO POPPERS

These are a classic American snack and they are best when battered and deep-fried, but can also be oven-fried—however, it is difficult to get the batter right if done in the oven. You can also deep-fry them completely without any batter if you want to avoid gluten, for example. If that's the case, deep-fry the poppers first, and then the fruits that are dipped in the flour and milk batter. Many wrap bacon strips around their poppers, which make them hold together better.

16 green jalapeños
3½ oz. (100 g.) cream cheese (Philadelphia style)
3½ oz. (100 g.) grated strong cheese Västerbotten cheese*
1/5 tsp (1 krm) grated lime zest
1 tsp lime juice
1 finely chopped chili, a red jalapeño for example
6¾ fl. oz. (2 dl.) all-purpose flour
6¾ fl. oz. (2 dl.) fine bread crumbs
bacon slices—optional
Canola or other neutral-tasting oil

Cut a slit lengthwise, from stem to the end, on one side of the jalapeño. Then cut a horizontal slit at the stem end to open the fruit and remove the seed. Work carefully to avoid splitting the fruits.

Mix the two cheeses with the lime juice and zest and the finely chopped chili. Fill each jalapeño with this filling. It's a bit tricky, so make it easier by using a teaspoon. Wrap the chili in a slice of bacon if you wish, and push a toothpick through the lot to make it hold together better.

Mix all-purpose flour and milk, and dip the fruits in this batter, and then in the bread crumbs. Heat the oil to 355°F (180°C)—preferably in a deep fat fryer if you have one—and deep-fry the jalapeños until they "pop" and are nicely colored. These should be eaten immediately.

TOM YUM

This is a classic Thai soup that can be made in several ways. It is difficult to omit the tamarind paste, as it gives the soup a tart flavor that balances the heat, the saltiness and the sweetness. You can add a few shrimp with the mushrooms if you like.

2 tbsp tamarind paste + 1 cup water
3 lemongrass stalks
approx. 1" (3 cm.) fresh ginger
3 shallots
1–2 Thai chilis, big Thai for example
3¼ cup (7½ dl.) water
1 tbsp soy sauce
2 tbsp fish sauce
3–4 kaffir lime leaves
1 tsp salt
1½ tbsp granulated sugar
1 14-oz. can coconut milk
15–20 mushrooms
3 salad onions
1 handful spinach or small mango leaves
a bunch of cilantro
½ lime

Place the tamarind paste in one cup of water and set aside. Peel and crush the lemongrass stalk and halve it. Finely chop the ginger, shallots and 1 chili. Cook these ingredients in water for about 10 minutes. Strain. Squeeze out the water from the tamarind paste and keep only the water. Pour the water into the stock along with the soy sauce, fish sauce, kaffir-lime leaves, salt, and sugar. Cook for about 5 minutes, and then add the coconut milk and let the soup cook for another 5 minutes. Taste. Quarter the mushrooms, slice the salad onions, and coarsely chop the spinach. Divide between 4 individual bowls. Pour the hot soup over and let steep for 5 minutes. Garnish with chopped cilantro and lime wedges, and perhaps a bit more finely chopped chili.

*Mature cheddar or Gruyère if Västerbotten isn't available.

TEXAS CHILI

serves 6–8

Authentic chili doesn't have ground beef, beans, or tomatoes but is made mainly with meat and chili. This version does have kidney beans, which have a full-bodied taste and help thicken the stew.

Step 1

4½ lbs (2 kg) chuck meat
butter for frying
2 tbsp smoked paprika powder
scant 1 lb (400 g.) celeriac
3½ oz. (100 g.) parsnip
1 large yellow onion
1 fruity chili, Rocoto or habanero for example
approx. 1½ quart (1½ liter) water

Trim the meat and cut it into 2"x2" cubes. Sear the meat on all sides in butter. Add paprika powder, and let it fry for a few minutes. Peel and chop the celeriac and parsnip coarsely. Cut the onion and the chili fruit into large wedges. Add the celeriac, parsnip, onion, and chili fruits to the meat and add water until everything is just covered. Bring it all to a boil and then turn down the heat to just a simmer. Let it simmer for 3–4 hours, or until the meat is fork tender.

Step 2

1 tbsp canola oil
3 shallots
2 or 3 chilis, Rocoto or habanero for example
3 garlic cloves
3 tbsp ground cumin
½ tbsp ground coriander
2–4 tsp ancho powder (smoked chili powder)
1 tbsp dried oregano
1 can kidney beans, 8¾ oz. (250 gr)
Stock from recipe's step 1
salt
black pepper

Take out the meat (from step 1) and set it aside. Blend the stock to make it "soupy." Finely chop the onions, 1 chili fruit, and the garlic. Fry this in oil in a separate saucepan. Add cumin, coriander, ancho powder, and oregano. Add about 3½ cup (8 dl.) of the stock from step 1 and let cook for 5–10 minutes. Season with salt and black pepper and maybe with some more fresh chili. Add the kidney beans and the meat, and add more stock if needed. Let it all simmer for about 5 minutes. Chili tastes better on day two and three, so it doesn't matter if you have leftovers. Serve with a nice loaf of bread, lime, and finely chopped chili.

5 SPECIES & 222 VARIETIES

There are just over 30 known species of the family *Capsicum* and thousands of cultivars. Spanish pepper, *C. annuum*, is the species with the most varieties (named hybrids/crossbreeds). You'll find, for example, cayenne and jalapeño in this group. Another four species are grown commercially and contain a number of cultivars: Berry-like pepper, *C. baccatum,* Tabasco pepper, *C. frutescens,* Havana pepper, *C. chinense*, and Rocoto pepper, *C. pubescens.* Habanero and the world's hottest chili, Carolina Reaper, belong to *C. chinense.* The Rocoto pepper differs most from the others in that it cannot be crossbred with other species, and its seeds are black. All five species are cultivars—they have been bred by humans and can't be found as true wild species.

There are still wild-growing species in South America, and they are occasionally picked and sold locally, even if the fruits are typically small and loaded with seeds. They usually have sprawling growth habits. As a rule, these wild species have no or few cultivars. Getting your hands on seeds from these wild species is tricky, but you can search online if you want to give it a try.

Capsicum microcarpum CAP_{253} is a cultivar from a wild species that is relatively easy to get hold of. It is reminiscent of *C. baccatum* and is sometimes registered as such. CAP_{253} is easy to cultivate and yields a generous harvest, and the fruits are tasty. In this chapter we'll present the five biggest and most well-known species—those that are also most grow-worthy and useful.

THE FINE ART OF CHOOSING

It can be very difficult to decide when there is a large selection of chili species and varieties. As a rookie it might feel safer to bet on a type you have tried earlier; one that had the right heat and you liked the flavor. That said, go ahead and test other varieties and species, as they have different growing habits and flavors, and other usages. You can try more and more varieties as you learn to grow and use chili in cooking. Wouldn't it be fun to try a chili that's from where you or your friends and family are from, or perhaps where you've gone on vacation? If you like the food from a certain country, choose chilis that are commonly grown there, perhaps for use in a special sauce or dish.

Sometimes space dictates what you can grow. It might be important, for example, to choose chili varieties that don't grow very tall, if they are to grow in a confined space like on a windowsill or out on a balcony. On the other hand, if you have plenty of space, it might be cool to grow a chili that grows tall. Check out the ornamental chilis, as they are often highly decorative.

Low-growing varieties:
Purple Tiger
Little Elf
NuMex Twilight
Superchili
Trinidad Bush

Tall varieties:
Brazilian Starfish
Dorset Naga
Jamaican Bell
Ethiopian Peppertree
Goat's Weed

We must of course talk about heat strength. As rookies, we're often cautious and choose chilis that are at about 1–3 on the scale (500–2,500 SHU), but go ahead and try some hotter varieties. Regular chili eaters consider types up to 6 (less than 30,000 SHU) as mild enough to use sliced in salads! Many types that register between 100,000 and 300,000 aren't just hot but also terrifically flavorful. To experience the flavor without all the spice, use the fruit like it is often used in India—pierce a hole in the fruit with a needle, place the fruit in the stew, and then fish it out when the there is enough heat.

Learning to appreciate different chili flavors and strengths is a question of you tasting all the different types out there. And don't forget to try your own homegrown chilis, both fresh and dried!

CAPSICUM MICROCARPUM CAP 253

Origin: El Salvador

Height: $3\frac{1}{4}$' (100 cm.)

Fruit: $2\frac{3}{4}$"–$3\frac{1}{5}$" (7cm.–8 cm.), oblong; red/orange

Strength/Heat: 6 (15,000–30,000 SHU)

Other/misc: CAP 253 is an unusual species. This one would be a lot of fun if you're interested in botany and want to grow many different types of chili

THIS IS HOW YOU INTERPRET THE INFORMATION IN THIS CHAPTER

We follow the spelling set down by the Swedish database for cultivated plants, as much as possible. Otherwise, we go with the common international spelling.

Origin: Town, country, or region where the chili originated.

Height: As high as the plant will grow if potted, in a greenhouse. Height varies depending on the size of the pot, care, and summer temperature.

Fruit: Size, shape, color—applies to ripe fruit.

Strength/heat: Heat is classified from 0–10+++ depending on how hot the chili is. The Scoville rating is in parenthesis.

Other: Other facts about the variety, such as if it is especially decorative or has specific usages.

SPANISH PEPPER

[CAPSICUM ANNUUM]

IN 1749 AN UNUSUAL plant was waving in the fields of Limhamn, outside the southern Swedish town of Malmö. Carl von Linnė, who at that time was touring the southern province of Skåne, was so impressed with this vegetable that he made note of it in his travelogue. As he understood it, after listening to the local farmers, this was an annual *Capsicum* that was grown so the farmers could add potency to the local aquavit, and Linnė gave the plant the name *annuum,* which means annual. What he didn't know is that chili is a perennial plant if grown in a tropical climate. A few years later the species' name was included in *Species plantarum*, and as such was accepted internationally, which means that confusion still reigns today. *Capsicum annuum* is quite simply a perennial plant that is grown as an annual in a cold climate.

C. annuum is the biggest and most variety-rich species within the family, with chilis that can stay as low as around 7¾" (20 cm.) or grow as high as 6½ feet (2 meters) in one season. Bell pepper belongs to the same family as chili, and they are both subgroups of *C. annuum.* Plants with sweet fruits are attributed to the bell pepper group and those with hot fruits to the chili pepper group. However, the border is fluid and it's not always easy to place the mild fruits in the right category.

The growth habit varies from tidy to sprawling; the leaves can be large or small, smooth or dented, green or purplish. The flowers are white, yellowy white, or lilac. The fruits vary in heat strength, size, color, form, and flavor. In this species you'll find ripe fruits in all the chili colors, even white, beige, lilac, and black. To pick out a *C. annuum,* the simplest way is to first rule out that the plant doesn't belong to one of the other of the four common species. Now, that isn't quite as easy as it sounds. For example, the jalapeño variety Farmers' Market is hairy, which is usually a characteristic for Rocoto peppers. On the other hand, Farmers' Market doesn't have black seeds and is therefore a *C. annuum*. To

Be careful when you water the sown seeds; do not water too little or overwater.

complicate things further, the *annum* varieties crossbreed both with each other and with varieties from the other species except *C. pubescens.*

Many varieties develop quickly, and are therefore good for beginning growers or anyone who cannot provide extra grow light. Even if it's advantageous to sow earlier, you can sow in February and still be able to harvest ripe fruit before the killing frost arrives.

The wax varieties are common in commercial growing because the waxy skin keeps the fruit attractive for a long time, which means they can handle longer times in transport to points of sale. These varieties have an extra thick and chewy skin, and they are usually medium hot. They are called Hungarian Hot Wax and Hungarian Wax Chili Pepper because they were bred in Hungary.

SOME FACTS ABOUT SPANISH PEPPER

Full plant development takes 4–7 months, depending on variety.
Sow: January–February
Strength/heat: 1–10 (100–800,000 SHU)
Other: There are very big variations between varieties, both in flavor, strength, looks, and development time.

The yellow wax peppers (such as Yellow Wax) have a skin that makes you think of beeswax. Santa Fe Grande is another much appreciated wax type. There are several kinds with large fruits and mild heat (1–2 on the scale) belonging to the *C. annuum* species. Anaheim and poblano are examples of mild wax peppers with large fruits. They're often used in dishes where they are stuffed with ground meat, cheese, or other fillings.

There is also another chili group within *C. annuum* that is officially called ornamental peppers, because that's just what they are. These especially decorative chili varieties have been bred because of their beautiful foliage and colorful fruits. The leaves are usually variegated or purplish. The fruits come in many different hues, and often grow simultaneously but at several stages of ripeness on the plant, which makes it look like all the colors of the rainbow are present. The spectacular colors are the result of the plant's anthocyanin content, which in tandem with certain sugars and pH levels produces a dark, lilac-tinged color. The same substance is present in blueberries, certain roses, and the copper beech. Many of these chili varieties are low-growing and are therefore excellent for a windowsill, but there are also a few taller ones growing to just under 3' (90 cm.). The fruits are completely edible, but often small and loaded with seeds, which makes it a real chore to clean them. The ornamental chili plants sold at garden centers are usually treated with plant-growth-regulating (PGR) hormones that inhibit growth to keep the plants low and manageable. These plants should be used solely as ornamentals. There is also a risk that ornamental chili is confused with the houseplant Jerusalem cherry, *Solanum pseudocapsicum,* which looks like an ornamental chili but is, in fact, poisonous.

AJI DE JARDIN

Origin: Cuba
Height: 1½' (45 cm.)
Fruit: ¾" (2 cm.) plump drop shape; red
Strength/heat: 6 (15,000–30,000 SHU)
Other: An ornamental plant with both upright and drooping fruits in lilac, orange, and red.

AMMAZZO

Origin: Italy
Height: 2'–3' (60 cm.–90 cm.)
Fruit: ¾" (2 cm.), globe shape; red
Strength/heat: 2 (1,000–1,500 SHU)
Other: Like the original chili plants, this one has upward-reaching round, small fruits, to attract birds. The birds will then eat the fruits and spread the seeds. This plant is also called Joe's Hot and Joe's Round.

ANAHEIM

Origin: New Mexico
Height: 2½'–3¼' (75 cm.–100 cm.)
Fruit: approx 6"–7" (15 cm.–18 cm.), plump drop shape; red
Strength: 2 (1,000–1,500 SHU)
Other: The farmer Emilio Ortega brought this American cultivar with him to Anaheim, California, at the beginning of the 20th century and named it after the community. The Anaheim is as big as a pointy bell pepper, juicy, and mild. Delicious when stuffed and fried, oven-baked, or grilled. The Anaheim is also called Magdalena or California chili. It can grow slightly hotter.

APACHE

Origin: United States
Height: approx. 1'–1½' (30 cm.–40 cm.)
Fruit: ¾"–2⅓" (2 cm.–6 cm.), oblong, plump; red
Strength/heat: 8 (80,000 SHU)
Other: Popular variety with beautiful shiny and meaty fruits and good flavor. The heat can vary from medium to fierce.

ARIZONA CHILTEPIN

Origin: US
Height: 1⅓' (40 cm.)
Fruit: ¾" (2 cm.), egg shape; red
Strength: 7 (30,000–50,000 SHU)
Other: Ornamental plant with dark foliage and black fruit that ripens to red.

AUSTRALIAN BROOME

Origin: Australia
Height: 1½'–2' (50 cm.–60 cm.)
Fruit: 2¾" (7 cm.), long, big with blunt end; red
Strength/heat: 9 (300,000 SHU)
Other: Rather big fruit that looks deceptively mild. This one can give quite a punch.

AURORA

Origin: US
Height: 6"–1' (15 cm.–30 cm.)
Fruit: ¾" (2 cm.), egg shape; red
Strength/heat: 7 (30,000–50,000 SHU)
Other: An ornamental chili. Low-growing plant and multicolored fruits. Would look lovely on the windowsill. Good heat.

BASKET OF FIRE F1

Origin: United Kingdom
Height: approx. 1'–1½' (30 cm.–50 cm.)
Fruit: 1½"–2⅓" (4 cm.–6 cm.), oblong; red
Strength/heat: 8 (80,000 SHU)
Other: Slightly pendulous growth habit that works well as a potted plant or in a hanging basket. Plenty of fruit that range from pale yellow to red. Thin skin and easy to dry.

BENI HIGHLANDS

Origin: Bolivia
Height: 2¼' (70 cm.)
Fruit: 2"–2⅓" (5 cm.–6 cm.), drop shape; yellow
Strength/heat: 7 (50,000 SHU)
Other: Looks a lot like a small slim lemon, but that's the only thing it has in common with the citrus.

BIG RED

Origin: Chile
Height: 2¼'–2⅔' (70 cm.–80 cm.)
Fruit: 3⅕"–3½" (8 cm.–9 cm.) oblong and curved; red
Strength/heat: 5 (5,000–10,000 SHU)
Other: Rumor has it that the fruit can grow much bigger, up to 8" (20 cm.), but we haven't seen this in our place. A fun shape, and it's enjoyable to have fruits that are simultaneously green and red. Plenty of fruit and good heat.

BIG THAI

Origin: Thailand
Height: 2¼'–2⅔' (70 cm.–8 cm.)
Fruit: 4" (10 cm.), very oblong; red
Strength/heat: 5 (5,000–15,000 SHU)
Other: Unusually elongated and slim, but otherwise a classic Thai chili with a slight bitter tang. Slim, tall plant and medium hot. It is called Chian Rai in Thailand, after a northern Thai province.

BLACK HUNGARIAN

Origin: Hungary
Height: 2⅔'–3¼' (80 cm.–100 cm.)
Fruit: 2"–2¾" (5 cm.–7 cm.), drop shape; red
Strength/heat; 5 (5,000–10,000 SHU)
Other: A jalapeño-type chili that is black as coal before turning reddish-brown and red. Can be eaten either black or red, and flavor and strength are close to other jalapeños. This one is sometimes called Hungarian Black. Flowers are lilac.

BLACK SCORPION TONGUE

Height: 2'–2¼' (60 cm.–70 cm.)
Fruit: 1½" (4 cm.), plump but the shape narrows; red
Strength/heat: 7 (50,000 SHU)
Other: Both plant and fruits are very beautiful. Even the leaves are attractive, and the plant grows bushy foliage that sometimes develops into a small tree. This plant is therefore suitable if you want to grow a bonsai chili. The fruit colors go from beige and yellow to lilac and red, and there are little stings growing on the end of the fruit. The plant generates lots of very tasty fruit. It can be eaten half-ripe without tasting bitter.

BLACK KNIGHT F1

Origin: Hungary
Height: 2' (60 cm.)
Fruit: 1¹/₅"–2" (3 cm.–5 cm.), plump, drop shape; red
Strength/heat: 8 (100,000 SHU)
Other: Dark foliage with fruits that go from green to black, and ripen to red.

BLUE CHRISTMAS

Height: 2'–3' (60 cm.–90 cm.)
Fruit: 2" (5 cm.), spool shape; red
Strength/heat: 6 (15,000–30,000 SHU)
Other: An ornamental plant with dark foliage and upright-pointing fruits that change color. This one is reminiscent of NuMex varieties from *C. chinense*, but belongs to *C. annuum*.

BOLIVIAN RAINBOW

Origin: Bolivia
Height: 1½' (50 cm.)
Fruit: ¾" (2 cm.), plump, drop shape; red
Strength/heat: 8 (50,000–100,000 SHU)
Other: An ornamental type with fruits in up to nine different hues such as lilac, yellow, and red. This one is suitable to make into a bonsai.

CALORO

Origin: Italy
Height: 2'–3' (60 cm.–90 cm.)
Fruit: 2"–2¾" (5 cm.–7 cm.), drop shape; red
Strength/heat: 4 (2,500–5,000 SHU)
Other: A very tasty and useful chili variety that can be eaten at every fruit stage, from unripe to ripe. The Caloro is mild enough to add to a salad.

CAP 1546

Origin: Bolivia
Height: $1^{2}/_{3}$' (50 cm.)
Fruit: $^{1}/_{3}$"–¾". (1 cm.–2 cm.), cone shape; red
Strength/heat: 7 (50,000 SHU)
Other: An ornamental chili with quite dark foliage and fruits in different hues of lilac, yellow, orange, and red. Would make an attractive bonsai.

CAYENNE

Cayenne is a classic chili fruit named after the French Guyana river Cayenne. The name comes from *quiyunha*, a word from the indigenous language. The fruit is oblong and slim, slightly bent, and shiny. The color varies between red, orange, and yellow. Cayenne Long Slim, Cayenne Golden, and Cayenne Picante are some varieties. A lot of cayenne is grown commercially in Africa, India, and Mexico and the southern United States. Dried cayenne pepper was already well known as a spice in 1795. The name cayenne is sometimes used as a collective name for all chilis.

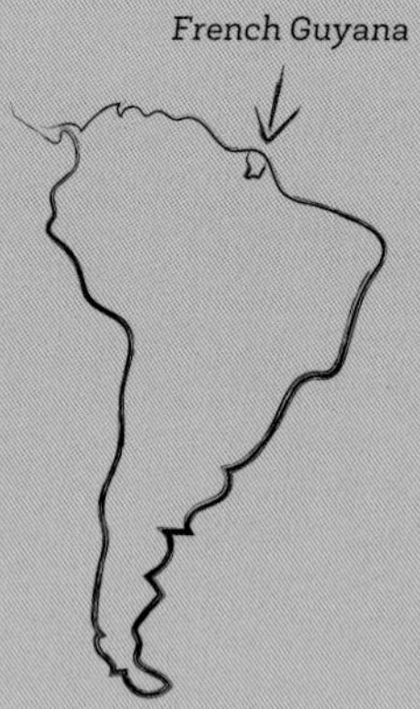

CAYENNE CAROLINA

Origin: US
Height: 2⅔'–3¼' (80 cm.–100 cm.)
Fruit: ¾"–1½" (2 cm.–4 cm.), oblong, slim; red
Strength/heat: 7 (30,000–50,000 SHU)
Other: A typical cayenne chili in both appearance and flavor. Cayenne Golden is a yellow variety of the same flavor, and it keeps its striking yellow color in both dried and powder form.

CAYENNE PICANTE

Origin: US
Height: 3'–3¼' (90 cm.–100 cm.)
Fruit: 2"–2¾" (5 cm.–7 cm.), oblong, slim; red
Strength/heat: 7 (40,000 SHU)
Other: This one sometimes produces decoratively hook-like fruits, and occasionally straight ones. This chili is perfect for drying and for grinding into powder. Good heat that doesn't overpower.

CHEYENNE ORANGE

Height: 1 1/3'–1 2/3' (40 cm.–50 cm.)
Fruit: 2"–2¾" (5–7 cm.) oblong and slim; stubby; yellow orange.
Strength: 7 (35,000 SHU)
Other: This variety produces lots of fruit even though the plant is quite low-growing. A beautiful chili with good flavor and fine heat.

CHILHUACLE NEGRO

Origin: Mexico
Height: 2'–2 1/4' (60 cm.–70 cm.)
Fruit: 1½"–2" (4 cm.–5 cm.), round; dark brown.
Strength/heat: 4 (2,500–5,000 SHU)
Other: Large fruits that have similar shape to Rocoto peppers, but this variety has thin skin. The flavor is smoky, which is good in a mole sauce. This chili can also be eaten fresh.

CHINESE 5-COLOR

Height: 2 1/4' (70 cm.)
Fruit: 1½" (4 cm.), drop shape; red
Strength: 7 (50,000 SHU)
Other: An ornamental chili with yellow, orange, red, and lilac fruits that poke up out of the plant. Dark-green foliage. The ripe fruit is red.

COLORADO PICANTE

Origin: US
Height: $2^2/_3$' (80 cm.)
Fruit: $3^1/_5$"–4" (8 cm.–10 cm.), oblong; red
Strength: 5 (5,000–10,000 SHU)
Other: This chili is reminiscent of a slim jalapeño and has the same somewhat meaty skin, which gives it a sturdy appearance. The growing habit is a bit like a *C. baccatum*, sprawling, high, and narrow with messy branches. It is very flavorful but not very hot.

CZECHOSLOVAKIAN BLACK

Origin: former Czechoslovakia
Height: 2' (60 cm.)
Fruit: 1½"–2" (4 cm.–5 cm.), drop shape; red
Strength/heat: 1 (1,000 SHU)
Other: This is a jalapeño-type chili with big meaty fruit. They start out black and ripen to red. Very mild.

ELEPHANT PEPPER

Origin: Macedonia
Height: $2^2/_3$'–$3^1/_4$' (80 cm.–100 cm.)
Fruit: approx. 6" (15 cm.) an oblong, sometimes twisted look, patterned; dark red.
Strength/heat: 4 (2,500–5,000 SHU).
Other: An old heirloom pepper from Macedonia, where it is called Vezena Piperka, which means "embroidered chili." Its stripes make it look like an elephant's trunk. This is a quite hard fruit, which makes it good for grilling. A bit bigger and a bit hotter than Elephant's Trunk.

ELEPHANT'S TRUNK

Origin: India
Height: $2^2/_3$'–$3^1/_4$' (80 cm.–100 cm.)
Fruit: 2"–3½" (5 cm.–9 cm.), oblong, slim, wrinkled, and curved like an elephant's trunk; red
Strength/heat: 2 (1,000–1,500 SHU)
Other: As the name implies, this chili looks like an elephant's trunk, same as the Elephant Pepper chili. Can look a bit dry on the surface. We've heard it can grow up to 6" (15 cm.) long.

ETNA

Origin: Italy
Height: approx. 7¾"–1½' (20 cm.–45 cm.)
Fruit: 7¾" (20 cm.), spool shape; red.
Strength/heat: 7 (30,000–50,000 SHU)
Other: This is an ornamental chili. The fruits grow in clusters and go from green to yellow, and ripen to red. They grow upward, which probably made the breeder think of the well-known volcano. A tidy and beautiful plant, suitable for the windowsill or balcony.

FACING HEAVEN

Origin: China
Height: 1⅔' (50 cm.)
Fruit: ⅔"–1½" (2 cm.–4 cm.) cone shape; red
Strength/heat: 7 (30,000–50,000 SHU)
Other: The fruits point up, which makes the plant look like an upward-stretching jalapeño. However, this chili's flavor is hotter. It is frequently used in Chinese cooking, where it's called Chao Tian Jiao.

FENIR

Origin: Czech Republic
Height: 2'–2¼' (60 cm.–70 cm.)
Fruit: 1½"–2" (4 cm.–5 cm.), pyramid shape; red.
Strength/heat: 2 (1,000 SHU)
Other: A beautifully shaped fruit that goes from green to orange to red. This one is mild.

FILIUS BLUE

Height: 1'–1 1/3' (30 cm.–40 cm.)
Fruit: 3/2"–1½" (2 cm.–4 cm.), round; red
Strength/heat: 7 (50,000 SHU)
Other: An ornamental variety with a beautiful growth habit and lilac and green variegated foliage. Even the stems and flowers are lilac. The fruits go from bluish lilac to yellow, orange, and then to red.

FISH PEPPER

Origin: Maryland
Height: 2'–3' (60 cm.–90 cm.)
Fruit: 1½"–2" (4 cm.–5 cm.), drop shape, stripy; red.
Strength/heat: 5 (5,000–15,000 SHU)
Other: This is one of the few stripy chilis, and lengthwise stripes are especially rare. This is an old heirloom, popular since the 19th century. Great with fish and shellfish dishes. Some traces of stripes can still be seen when the fruit turns red. The foliage is also variegated.

FRESNO

Origin: US
Height: 2 1/4' (70 cm.)
Fruit: 2"–2 1/3" (5 cm.–6 cm.), plump, drop shape; red.
Strength/heat: 4 (2,500–5,000 SHU)
Other: A jalapeño-type chili both in flavor and appearance. Introduced in 1952, it is often used in ceviche and in salsa. This is a common variety in the United States. The chili is meaty and needs to be dried in the oven or in a dehydrator.

FRIGGITELLO

Origin: Italy
Height: 2'–3' (60 cm.–90 cm.)
Fruit: $3^1/_5$"–4" (8 cm.–10 cm.), drop shape; red
Strength/heat: 1 (100 SHU)
Other: This is the Italian equivalent of Padrón, which is often eaten green. It is a mild chili, and in contrast to Padrón you'll never get any hot fruits off this plant. An old Naples heirloom that is very popular as antipasto when sautéed in oil. Let the fruit ripen to red if you want to collect its seed.

GOAT'S WEED

Origin: Venezuela
Height: $3^1/_4$'–4' (100 cm.–120 cm.)
Fruit: $2^1/_3$" (6 cm.), oblong; red.
Strength/heat: 7 (30,000–50,000 SHU)
Other: Upright fruit. Fruit is green, turns black and red, and looks a little like a goat's horns, which probably is the origin of the name. The stems are somewhat hairy, almost velvety. Sprawling growth habit similar to that of *C. baccatum*.

HINKELHATZ YELLOW

Origin: US
Height: 2' (60 cm.)
Fruit: ¾"–$1^1/_5$" (2 cm.–3 cm.), plump, blunt end; red/orange.
Strength/heat: 6 (15,000–30,000 SHU)
Other: A little bit odd-looking, like a slim habanero, and with mild flavor. Unusually attractive stem attachment. Chicken Heart is another name for the red Hinkelhatz.

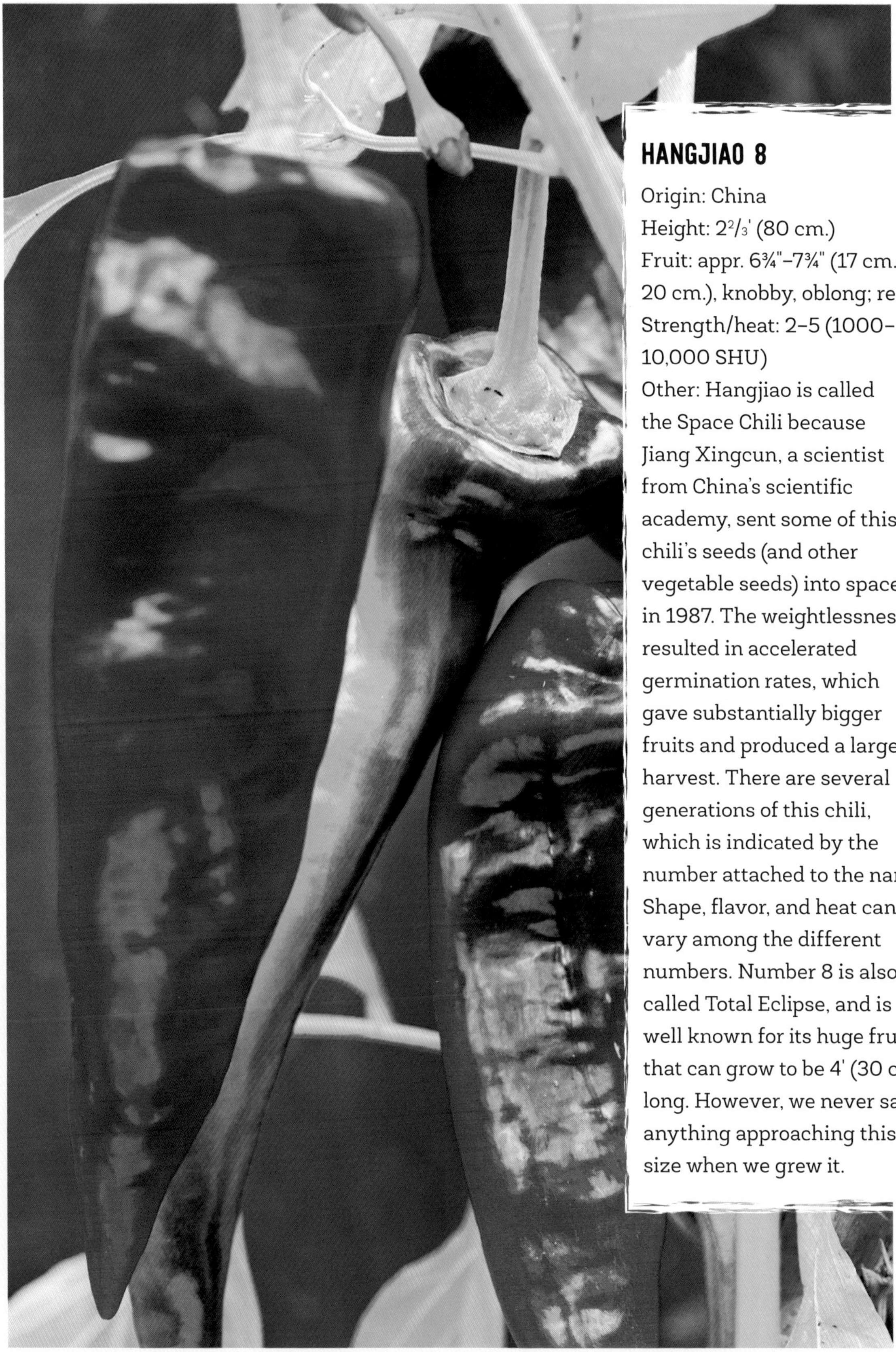

HANGJIAO 8

Origin: China
Height: 2⅔' (80 cm.)
Fruit: appr. 6¾"–7¾" (17 cm.–20 cm.), knobby, oblong; red
Strength/heat: 2–5 (1000–10,000 SHU)
Other: Hangjiao is called the Space Chili because Jiang Xingcun, a scientist from China's scientific academy, sent some of this chili's seeds (and other vegetable seeds) into space in 1987. The weightlessness resulted in accelerated germination rates, which gave substantially bigger fruits and produced a larger harvest. There are several generations of this chili, which is indicated by the number attached to the name. Shape, flavor, and heat can vary among the different numbers. Number 8 is also called Total Eclipse, and is well known for its huge fruits that can grow to be 4' (30 cm.) long. However, we never saw anything approaching this size when we grew it.

HONG GOCHU

Origin: Korea
Height: $2\frac{2}{3}$'–$3\frac{1}{4}$' (80 cm.–100 cm.)
Fruit: $3\frac{1}{5}$"–4" (8 cm.–10 cm.), oblong; red
Strength/heat: 3 (1,500–2,500 SHU)
Other: A classic Korean chili that is used in the national dish, kimchi. *Gochu* is the Korean word for chili. Chili paste made from Hong Gochu is called *gochujang*, and the dried powder's name is *gochugaru*.

HOT PALETTE

Height: approx. 9¾" (25 cm.)
Fruit: 1½"–2" (4 cm.–5 cm.), oblong, pointed; red
Strength/heat: 6
(15,000–30,000 SHU)
Other: A small decorative plant with variegated foliage in green and white and fruit that go from pale yellow to yellow, orange, and red. Flavor and heat are similar to a medium-hot Thai chili.

HUNGARIAN YELLOW WAX

Origin: Hungary
Height: 2' (60 cm.)
Fruit: 4¾"–6" (12 cm.–15 cm.), plump, drop shape; red.
Strength/heat: 4 (2,500–5,000 SHU)
Other: The waxy skin gives the fruit an enamel-like shine. The fruits are relatively thin-skinned to be so big. They ripen from green to yellow and then to red.

JALAPEÑO

Jalapeño is one of the world's most recognized chili fruits. It originated in Mexico and it is named after the town Xalapa, but is often called *Cuaresmenoa* by the Mexicans. Fresh jalapeño is a must with nachos and other Mexican dishes. The jalapeño is recognized by its $2\frac{3}{4}$"–$3\frac{1}{5}$" (7 cm.–8 cm.)-long fruits, which are unusually meaty for a chili. Its skin is often very shiny and beautiful.

There is a long line of different jalapeño cultivars, for example the Jalapeño Black, which of course is black. There is Jalapeño Purple, which turns lilac, and Jalapeño Orange, which ripens to orange. Jalapeños are often harvested unripe to be put into brines for pickles, or to be filled with cheese to become jalapeño poppers.

Some jalapeño varieties get cracks in their skin's surface toward the end of the ripening stage—this is called corking. Corking doesn't harm the chilis, and some growers even feel that it adds an extra attractive touch. Varieties that are known for their decorative corking are the Jalapeño Farmers' Market and Jalapeño Cracked. American growers have bred hardy and mild varieties—NuMex Jalmundo is one—to sell as snacks at different sporting events.

When a jalapeño is smoked, its name changes to chipotle. There are two versions of chipotle; one is a green, heavily smoked fruit that gets a matte, almost grayish color. It is called Meco, Ahumado, or Tipico. Morita is the other version, and it is lightly smoked, shiny, and dark lilac jalapeño.

JALAPEÑO CRACKED

Origin: Mexico
Height: 2¼'–2⅔' (70 cm.–80 cm.)
Fruit: 2"–2⅓" (5 cm.–6 cm.) plump, blunt end; red
Strength/heat: 5 (5,000–10,000 SHU)
Other: Unusually blunt-ended to be a jalapeño, but just as tasty and mild. This chili is known for its corking, which happens at the end of the ripening process. Each fruit ripens from the bottom up, which makes it look very nice.

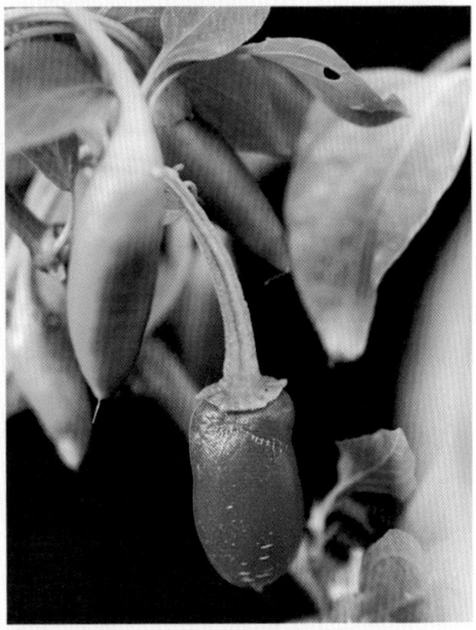

JALAPEÑO CRAIG'S GRANDE

Origin: US
Height: 2¼'–3' (70 cm.–90 cm.)
Fruit: 2"–4" (5 cm.–10 cm.), plump, drop shape, blunt end; red
Strength/heat: 5 (5,000 SHU)
Other: A big jalapeño chili with faint corking. This chili is mild and useful for poppers or pickles.

JALAPEÑO FARMERS' MARKET

Origin: US
Height: 2'–3' (60 cm.–90 cm.)
Fruit: 2⅓"–3⅕" (6 cm.–8 cm.), plump, with crazing/corking; red
Strength/heat: 5 (5,000–10,000 SHU)
Other: Much-enjoyed variety with lots of corking, which sometimes makes it more potato-colored than red. This one is also called Market Potato or Potato Jalapeño.

JALAPEÑO M

Origin: Mexico
Height: 2¼' (70 cm.)
Fruit: 2"–2$^{1}/_{3}$" (5 cm.–6 cm.), plump; red
Strength/heat: 5 (5,000 SHU)
Other: This variety is supposed to produce more fruit in a cooler climate than other jalapeños. In other respects it is very much like the traditional jalapeño. It can be eaten both green and red.

JALAPEÑO MAMMOTH

Origin: US
Height: 2'–3' (60 cm.–90 cm.)
Fruit: 2"–2¾" (5 cm.–7 cm.), plump, drop shape; red
Strength/heat: 5 (5,000 SHU)
Other: This chili is usually used while still green, but the flavor develops nicely if it is left to ripen until red. Mild and delicious flavor.

JALAPEÑO NEW MEXICO NO 8

Origin: US
Height: 2'–3' (60 cm.–90 cm.)
Fruit: 2"–2$^{1}/_{3}$" (5 cm.–6 cm.) plump; red
Strength/heat: 5 (5,000–10,000 SHU)
Other: A modern jalapeño variety from the Chile Pepper Institute in New Mexico.

JALAPEÑO ORANGE

Origin: Mexico
Height: 2$^{2}/_{3}$' (80 cm.)
Fruit: 2¾"–3$^{1}/_{5}$" (7 cm.–8 cm.), plump, drop shape; orange
Strength/heat: 4 (5,000 SHU)
Other: A bit slimmer and more pointy than most jalapeños. Fine, mild flavor and beautiful coloring.

JALAPEÑO PURPLE

Origin: Mexico
Height: 3¼'–4' (100 cm.–120 cm.)
Fruit: 3¼'–4' (100 cm.–120 cm.) drop-shaped, plump; red
Strength/heat: 5 (5,000–10,000 SHU)
Other: The fruit goes from green to a blackish lilac color before ripening to red. Reminiscent of Black Jalapeño but becomes wine red when ripe. This chili is eaten both black and unripe, and when red and ripe.

JALAPEÑO SEÑORITA

Origin: US
Height: 3¼'–4' (100 cm.–120 cm.)
Fruit: 2"–2¾" (5 cm.–7 cm.), plump; red
Strength/heat: 5 (5,000–15,000 SHU)
Other: A bit smaller and plumper than other jalapeños. Might develop some corking.

JIMMY NARDELLO

Origin: Italy
Height: 3¼' (100 cm.)
Fruit: 4"–4¾" (10 cm.–12 cm.), oblong, pointed; red
Strength/heat: 0 (›100 SHU)
Other: Chili flavor without any heat. Early fruit might twist, but they grow beautifully long and straight later in the season. The seeds were brought to the United States by Giuseppe and Angela Nardello when they emigrated from Italy to Connecticut in 1887. They brought chili seeds for a chili that would be named Jimmy, after their fourth son. An old heirloom. This chili is equally good grilled as in salad.

KALI MIRCH

Origin: India
Height: 3¼' (100 cm.)
Fruit: 2¾"–4" (7 cm.–10 cm.), oblong, pointed; dark red
Strength/heat: 6 (30,000 SHU)
Other: The fruits go from deliciously enamel black to red when they are ripe. Partly dark foliage, which darkens the more daylight it receives.

KOREAN HOT

Origin: Korea
Height: 1 1/3' (40 cm.)
Fruit: 1½"–2" (4 cm.–5 cm.), plump, drop shape; red
Strength/heat: 6 (15,000–30,000 SHU)
Other: Common in Korean cuisine and perfect for making kimchi. A very prolific chili.

LAVA CARIBE

Height: 4'–1 1/3' (30 cm.–40 cm.)
Fruit: 3 1/5"–4" (8 cm.–10 cm.), drop shape; red
Strength/heat: 2 (1,000–1,500 SHU)
Other: The fruits are so beautiful that this plant could be called ornamental, but the fruits are much larger, very tasty, and fruity. With a bit of luck the fruits will turn tricolored—red, yellow, and orange—while ripening, which gives the fruit a "blazing" appearance.

LITTLE ELF

Origin: Mexico
Height: 1½' (45 cm.)
Fruit: 1/3"–2/3" (1 cm.–2 cm.), drop shape; red
Strength/heat: 6 (30,000 SHU)
Other: An ornamental chili with upward-pointing fruits that start out white and then change over to yellow, lilac, and red. A very beautiful plant with fine foliage that is excellent as a decorative potted plant.

LOMBARDO

Origin: Lombardy, Italy
Height: 3¼'–4' (100 cm.–120 cm.)
Fruit: 4"–6" (10 cm.–15 cm.), oblong, twisted; red
Strength/heat: 1 (1,00–1,000 SHU)
Other: A decorative fruit. A mild snack chili used in salads or as garnish for a stew. This chili is also good grilled. In Italy it's used to make pickled pepperoncini.

MARISOL

Origin: Spain
Height: $1^{2}/_{3}$' (50 cm.)
Fruit: 3½"–4¾" (9 cm.–12 cm.), spool shape; red
Strength/heat: 6 (15,000–30,000 SHU)
Other: When dried this chili is called guajillo. The same name might also be found on seed lists, but the correct name for the plant is Marisol. A traditional Spanish chili, popular in Spanish cooking, especially when dried.

MAZARONI RIVER

Origin: Guyana
Height: 4'–$1^{1}/_{3}$' (30 cm.–50 cm.)
Fruit: $1^{1}/_{5}$"–2" (3 cm.–5 cm.), plump, drop shape; red
Strength/heat: 7–8 (30,000–70,000 SHU)
Other: An orchid hunter discovered this chili at the river Mazaroni in Guyana. It is excellent in a hanging basket because it produces lots of fruit that weigh down the branches, giving the plant a pendant look.

MONKEY FACE RED

Origin: Oaxaca, Mexico
Height: 2'–3' (60 cm.–90 cm.)
Fruit: 4"–6" (10 cm.–15 cm.), variable shapes; red
Strength/heat: 4 (2,500–5,000 SHU)
Other: The fruits vary a lot in appearance, but enough of them remind you of monkey faces to give the variety its name. In contrast to its red counterpart, the yellow version of Monkey Face doesn't always get the typical "monkey face," but can still surprise you with different shapes.

MULATO ISLENO

Origin: Mexico
Height: 2'–3' (60 cm.–90 cm.)
Fruit: 3⅕"–4" (8 cm.–10 cm.) broad, plump, drop shape; brown
Strength/heat: 2 (1,000–15,000 SHU)
Other: Beautiful fruit in a bell pepper shape, which is often used dried in Mexican cooking to make mole sauce, for example. Very closely related to the Poblano. It is called ancho when dried; however, ancho is originally made from the poblano.

MUSHROOM YELLOW

Origin: Jamaica
Height: 2' (60 cm.)
Fruit: 1½"–2" (4 cm.–5 cm.), plump with ridges; yellow-orange
Strength/heat: 8 (50,000–100,000 SHU)
Other: The fruits grow in bunches, many fruits together. It's fiery and very tasty. This chili is probably a crossbreed with *C. chinense*, as the fruits have that appearance. This chili is also sold as Yellow Mushroom CAP and Jamaican Mushroom Yellow.

NUMEX BAILEY PIQUIN

Origin: New Mexico
Height: 2⅔'–3' (80 cm.–90 cm.)
Fruit: ¾"–1⅕" (2 cm.–3cm.), oblong; red
Strength/heat: 8 (50,000–100,000 SHU)
Other: This one is quite hot for a NuMex chili. The foliage turns beautifully dark green and gets darker as the season goes on.

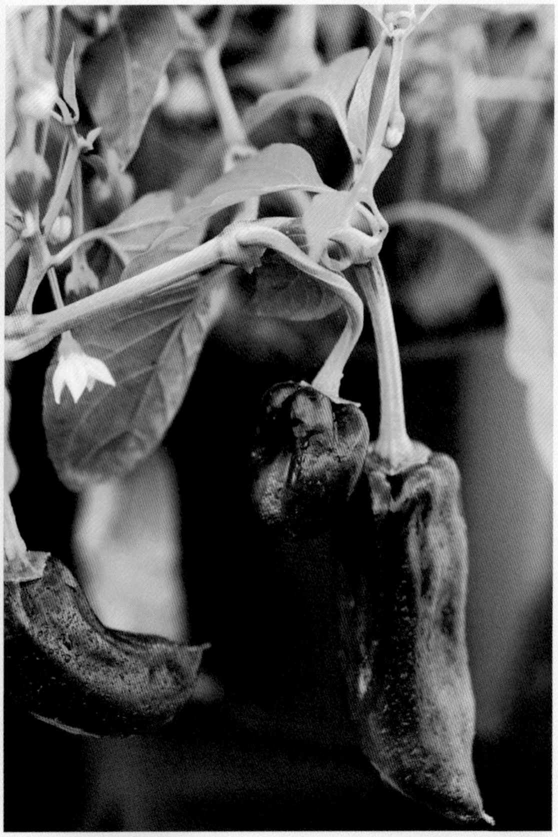

NUMEX CENTENNIAL

Origin: New Mexico
Height: 3'–4' (90 cm.–120 cm.)
Fruit: 1/3"–2/3" (1 cm.–2 cm.) globe shape; red
Strength/heat: 4 (5,000 SHU)
Other: This is an ornamental variety. The fruit aren't much bigger than peas; they start out green and then turn black and finally to red.

NUMEX ECLIPSE

Origin: New Mexico
Height: 1 1/3' (40 cm.)
Fruit: 4"–4¾" (10 cm.–12 cm.) drop shape that comes to a point; brown
Strength/heat: 1 (300–500 SHU)
Other: An ornamental chili with big, beautifully brown fruit on a small plant. This one, along with NuMex Sunset and NuMex Sunrise, are bred at the University of New Mexico to be especially suitable for *ristras*, bunches of dried chilis to be suspended for decoration and as a symbol of hospitality and happiness.

NUMEX ESPANHOLA

Origin: New Mexico
Height: 3' (90 cm.)
Fruit: 3 1/5"–4" (8 cm.–10 cm.), plump; red
Strength/heat: 3 (1,500–2,500 SHU)
Other: A mild jalapeño type that ripens into a dark red-brown color.

NUMEX JOE E. PARKER

Origin: New Mexico
Height: 3' (90 cm.)
Fruit: 3 1/5"–4" (8 cm.–10 cm.), plump, drop shape; red
Strength/heat: 4 (2,500–4000 SHU)
Other: A mild jalapeño type.

NUMEX PRIMAVERA JALAPEÑO

Origin: New Mexico
Height: 2'–3' (60 cm.–90 cm.)
Fruit: 2"–2¾" (5 cm.–7 cm.), plump; red
Strength/heat: 5 (8,000 SHU)
Other: Slight corking—a nice modern jalapeño variety.

NUMEX TWILIGHT

Origin: New Mexico
Height: 4' (30 cm.)
Fruit: ¾" (2 cm.), drop shape; red
Strength/heat: 8 (50,000 SHU)
Other: An ornamental variety with upward-pointing fruit that go from pale yellow to lilac, and then turn to orange and red.

OROZCO

Origin: Eastern Europe
Height: 3' (90 cm.)
Fruit: 1¹/₅"–2" (3 cm.–5 cm.), spool shape; red
Strength/heat: 4 (5,000 SHU)
Other: An ornamental chili with small fruit that go from green to brownish lilac, to black and yellow, until ripening in orange and red. Beautiful dark foliage. This chili is popular in Turkish cuisine.

PADRÓN

Origin: Spain
Height: $2\frac{2}{3}$' (80 cm.)
Fruit: 2"–$3\frac{1}{5}$" (5 cm.–8 cm.), plump, blunt end; red
Strength/heat: 1–5 (5,000–15,000 SHU)
Other: A very popular variety that is often served grilled as tapas in Spain. However, among all the mild fruit, sometimes a very strong one turns up, so it can be a bit of Russian roulette to take a bite out of a Padrón. Sometimes the fruit is called Pimiento de Padrón, but that is the name of the dish, not the chili variety.

PELLEGRINO

Origin: Italy
Height: 1⅔' (50 cm.)
Fruit: 1⅕"–1 2/" (3 cm.–4 cm.), plump, blunt end; red
Strength/heat: 1 (900 SHU)
Other: A traditional Italian variety with low heat. Upward-growing plants that almost look like they have been "topped."

PEPPERONI DE EUSEBIO

Origin: Tenerife, Spain
Height: 3¼' (100 cm.)
Fruit: 3⅕"–3½" (8 cm.–9 cm.) plump and pointy; red
Strength/heat: 5 (5000–15,000 SHU)
Other: A beautiful fruit with a small fold near the stem attachment. Mild, good flavor. This chili is also called Aji Picante de Eusebio.

PETER PEPPER RED

Origin: US
Height: 2¼'–3' (70 cm.–90 cm.)
Fruit: 2¾"–4" (7 cm.–10 cm.) plump, red
Strength/heat: 6 (15,000–23,000 SHU)
Other: This one is popular because some fruit look somewhat like a penis. However, to be honest, the shape can vary a lot, and sometimes you'll need a very vivid imagination to make the association. A curiosity known under names such as Red Peter, Penis Chili, and Willie Chili. The pepper exists in yellow and orange as Peter Pepper Yellow and Peter Pepper Orange.

PETIT MARSEILLAIS

Origin: France
Height: 2'–3' (60 cm.–90 cm.)
Fruit: 2⅓"–3⅕" (6 cm.–8 cm.), long and plump; golden yellow
Strength/heat: 2 (1,000–1,500 SHU)
Other: Not quite so "petite" (small) but a big chili with only a little bit of heat. A perfect chili for those who don't want or can't tolerate a lot of heat. Good fruity flavor.

PIMENTA DE LA PUTA LA MADRE

Origin: Canary Islands, Spain
Height: 3' (90 cm.)
Fruit: ¾"–$1\frac{1}{5}$" (2 cm.–3 cm.), spool shape; red
Strength/heat: 9 (100,000–350,000 SHU)
Other: The name is a very coarse Spanish expression, but the heat isn't all that big. A quite meaty fruit that ripens from green to yellow, and then to red.

PIMENT D'ESPELETTE

Origin: France
Height: $1\frac{1}{3}$'–$2\frac{2}{3}$' (40 cm.–80 cm.)
Fruit: $1\frac{1}{5}$"–2¾" (3 cm.–7 cm.) oblong; red
Strength/heat: 4 (4,000 SHU)
Other: This is France's most popular and most frequently grown chili, and its ancestry dates back to the 16th century. Its fruit is very flavorful. The dried powder is often used to replace pepper, even though it's quite mild. Espelette is in the Basque region of France, on the slopes of the Pyranees. The growing conditions allow for ripe fruits between August and December. There are strict regional rules on how to grow the chili, and the use of pesticides is strictly regulated. The fruits are dried, ground, and then smoked.

PINOCCHIO'S NOSE

Origin: Italy
Height: 3¼' (100 cm.)
Fruit: $3\frac{1}{5}$"–4" (8 cm.–10 cm.), oblong and pointed; red
Strength/heat: 7 (50,000 SHU)
Other: When at its best, the fruit reminds you of Pinocchio's long nose, but sometimes the fruit grows a bit shorter.

POBLANO

Origin: Mexico
Height: $2\frac{1}{4}$' (70 cm.)
Fruit: $2\frac{3}{4}$"–4" (7 cm.–10 cm.) plump, irregular shape; red
Strength/heat: 2 (1,000–1,500 SHU)
Other: A very popular, big, bell pepper-shaped chili with low heat. It's often harvested green and filled with different types of stuffing, but it is also used in mole sauce. The poblano's name changes to ancho when the poblano is dried, and occasionally the seeds are sold under the wrong name, ancho.

PRAIRIE FIRE

Origin: Mexico
Height: $7\frac{3}{4}$" (20 cm.)
Fruit: $1\frac{1}{5}$" (3 cm.) drop shape; red
Strength/heat: 8 (70,000 SHU)
Other: An ornamental variety, with fruits in many different colors ranging from lilac to yellow, orange, and red. Upright-growing fruit.

PURIRA

Origin: Mexico
Height: $1\frac{2}{3}$' (50 cm.)
Fruit: $1\frac{1}{2}$"–$2\frac{1}{3}$" (4 cm.–6 cm.) plump; red
Strength/heat: 8 (50,000–100,000 SHU)
Other: A small plant, perfect for the windowsill or balcony. The fruit starts out green, and then turns yellow and finally red.

PURPLE FLASH

Origin: US
Height: 13¾" (35 cm.)
Fruit: ¾"–1⅕" (2 cm.–3 cm.), round; red
Strength/heat: 5 (5,000–6,000 SHU)
Other: An ornamental variety with round, globe-like fruits that are dark lilac before they are ripe. It has variegated foliage in light and dark lilac hues.

PURPLE SERRANO

Origin: Mexico
Height: 1⅔'–2⅔' (50 cm.–80 cm.)
Fruit: 1½"–2" (4 cm.–5 cm.), smooth and plump; dark red
Strength/heat: 6 (20,000 SHU)
Other: This one is reminiscent of a jalapeño both in appearance and flavor, but is a bit hotter. First the fruit is green, then black, and finishes in a nice dark red color when ripe. The name serrano indicates that the chili originated in the highlands—*serrano* is the Portuguese word for highland.

PURPLE TIGER

Origin: US
Height: 1⅓' (40 cm.)
Fruit: 1½" (4 cm.), plump drop shape; red
Strength/heat: 4 (5,000 SHU)
Other: An ornamental variety with variegated foliage in green, white, and lilac. The fruits stay lilac a long time before they ripen to red. Slightly pendant growth habit, which makes the plant well suited for hanging baskets. This chili is also called Purple Variegata and Trifetti.

PURPLE UFO

Height: 2¼' (70 cm.)
Fruit: 2" (5 cm.), blunt cone shape; red
Strength/heat: 7 (50,000 SHU)
Other: This beautifully formed fruit gets its name because it stays lilac for a long time before ripening to red. Maybe its shape also looks a little like a UFO.

QUINDILLA BLANCA

Origin: Spain
Height: 1⅔'–2⅔' (50 cm.–80 cm.)
Fruit: 2¾ "–4" (7 cm.–10 cm.) oblong; red
Strength/heat: 3 (1,500–2,500 SHU)
Other: This one goes directly from red to green. Delicious when grilled, and makes good tapas. This chili is also known as Quindilla.

RED HOT ODESSA

Origin: Ukraine
Height: 2⅔' (80 cm.)
Fruit: 4¾"–6" (12 cm.–15 cm.) oblong; red
Strength/heat: 4 (2,500–5,000 SHU)
Other: This is an old variety named after the Ukrainian harbor town Odessa. It can vary quite a lot in strength.

ROOSTER SPUR

Origin: US
Height: $1^{1}/_{3}$'–2' (40 cm.–60 cm.)
Fruit: ¾"–2" (2 cm.–5 cm.) spool shape; red
Strength/heat: 9 (170,000 SHU)
Other: A small nice chili plant with tiny upward pointing fruits that look a bit like the spur on a rooster's foot. These are perfect to add whole to a stew. Remove them once the flavor is strong enough for the dish.

ROYAL BLACK

Height: $1^{2}/_{3}$' (50 cm.)
Fruit: ¾" (2 cm.), round; red
Strength/heat: 6 (15,000–30,000 SHU)
Other: An ornamental variety with many pea-sized fruits that start out black but ripen to red. The foliage is dark.

SANTA FE GRANDE

Origin: Mexico
Height: 2'–3' (60 cm.–90 cm.)
Fruit: 2"–$2^{1}/_{3}$" (5 cm.–6 cm.), plump, drop shape; red
Strength/heat: 4 (2,500–5,000 SHU)
Other: Reminiscent of a large mild Hungarian wax, and is counted as one of the wax varieties. The fruits start out yellow, then turn green, and then ripen to red.

SARIT GAT

Origin: Kosovo
Height: 1²/₃' (50 cm.)
Fruit: 4"–4¾" (10 cm.–12 cm.), oblong, drop shape; yellow
Strength/heat: 7 (50,000 SHU)
Other: Beautiful fruit shape and wonderful yellow color that can, however, turn brown if the fruit is left too long on the plant. Nice to dry, as it retains its yellow color. This chili is thin-skinned and ripens early.

SATAN'S KISS

Origin: Italy
Height: 1²/₃' (50 cm.)
Fruit: ¾"–1¹/₅" (2 cm.–3 cm.), globe shape; red
Strength/heat: 7 (30,000–50,000 SHU)
Other: Amusing fruit shape that has room for quite a lot of seeds. Nice to scoop out, and fill with cream cheese. This one is also called Chiliega Piccante.

SERRANO

Origin: Mexico
Height: 3' (90 cm.)
Fruit: 2"–2¾" (5 cm.–7 cm.), plump, straight; red
Strength/heat: 6 (15,000–25,000 SHU)
Other: A jalapeño type named after the mountains in Puebla and Hidalgo in Mexico. Somewhat hotter than the regular jalapeño. Dried serrano is called Seco.

SUPERCHILI

Height: 1½' (45 cm.)
Fruit: 2"–2¾" (5 cm.–7 cm.) drop shape; red
Strength/heat: 7 (40,000–50,000 SHU)
Other: This plant produces tons of fruit. Grows with upward-pointing fruit, which appear above the foliage in colors as varied as near white to pale yellow, orange, and red. Beautiful as a potted plant.

SWEET BANANA

Origin: US
Height: 2' (60 cm.)
Fruit: 6"–7¾" (15 cm.–20 cm.) oblong; yellow
Strength/heat: 5 (5,000–15,000 SHU)
Other: This one is named for its appearance. It's an old heirloom in the United States. Might need to be harvested regularly to encourage new bud production.

TENNESSEE TEARDROPS

Origin: US
Height: 2'–$2^{2}/_{3}$' (60 cm.–80 cm.)
Fruit: 2"–$2^{1}/_{3}$" (5 cm.–6 cm.), oblong, drop shape; red
Strength/heat: 6 (15,000–30,000 SHU)
Other: Fruit color goes from yellow to orange, to lilac and red, which makes for a very beautiful plant.

TEQUILA SUNRISE

Origin: Mexico
Height: $1^{2}/_{3}$' (50 cm.)
Fruit: $2^{1}/_{3}$"–2¾" (6 cm.–7 cm.), oblong; yellow
Strength/heat: 4 (5,000 SHU)
Other: The fruits point straight out from the stems, but the branches dip down from the weight if there's a lot of fruit.

THAI HOT CULINARY

Origin: Thailand
Height: 2'–2$^2/_3$' (60 cm.–80 cm.)
Fruit: 1$^1/_5$"–1½" (3 cm.–4 cm.) oblong; red
Strength/heat: 6 (15,000–30,000 SHU)
Other: Fine Thai chili with a slight tart edge. Not too hot.

THAI ORANGE HOT

Origin: Thailand
Height: 3'–3¼' (90 cm.–100 cm.)
Fruit: 2$^1/_3$"–2¾" (6 cm.–7 cm.) slim, pointed; orange
Strength/heat: 8 (50,000–80,000 SHU)
Other: A tree-like plant with a proper 'crown', which is bushy and produces lots of fruit. A staple ingredient in Thailand, its homeland.

TRICOLOR VARIEGATA

Origin: Mexico
Height: 1'–1½' (30 cm.–45 cm.)
Fruit: 1$^1/_5$"–2" (3 cm.–5 cm.) plump; red
Strength/heat: 7 (50,000 SHU)
Other: An ornamental variety with beautifully variegated foliage in green, white, and lilac. The fruit also shows three colors on the same plant: lilac, orange yellow, and red.

TRINIDAD BUSH

Origin: Trinidad and Tobago
Height: 1'–1⅓' (30 cm.–40 cm.)
Fruit: 1½"–2" (4 cm.–5 cm.), oblong; red
Strength/heat: 6 (30,000 SHU)
Other: Low-growing plant with a slightly pendant growth habit, which makes it suitable for a hanging basket. Fine, medium-hot variety, which ripens early in the season.

URFA BIBER

Origin: Turkey
Height: 2⅔'–3' (80 cm.–90 cm.)
Fruit: 1½"–2" (4 cm.–5 cm.), plump, knobby; brownish red
Strength/heat: 3 (1,500–2,500 SHU)
Other: This varietal's name seems to be common to a lot of different types of Turkish chilis, but this one is probably the most accurate plant. In Turkey, this chili is fried and eaten for breakfast; the taste is a bit smoky, sweet, and mild. The color goes from brownish red to chestnut color.

VAMPIRE

Height: 2'–2¼' (60 cm.–70 cm.)
Fruit: ½"–2" (4 cm.–5 cm.), drop shape; red
Strength/heat: 5 (14,000 SHU)
Other: A decorative plant with dark green foliage and fruits that—using a bit of imagination—look like vampire teeth. It's a relatively mild chili, so it isn't named for its bite. The fruit turns from green to black and then to red.

VECTURA YELLOW

Height: 2'–2¼' (60 cm.–70 cm.)
Fruit: 2$\frac{1}{3}$"–3$\frac{1}{5}$" (6 cm.–8 cm.) oblong; yellow
Strength/heat: 6 (15,000–30,000 SHU)
Other: A cayenne-style chili with yellow fruit. This chili is used in Indian and Asian cuisine.

VOLCANO

Height: 2¼'–3' (70 cm.–90 cm.)
Fruit: 4"–4¾" (10 cm.–12 cm.), oblong; red
Strength/heat: 4 (2,500–5,000 SHU)
Other: Long fruits that are delicious when grilled. The fruits are pale green at first and then turn yellow, orange, and finally red. There are mentions of even bigger fruits, measuring up to 9¾" (25 cm.).

WENK'S YELLOW HOT

Origin: New Mexico
Height: 2¼'–2⅔' (70 cm.–80 cm.)
Fruit: 2"–2¾" (5 cm.–7 cm.) plump with a small sting growing at the end; red
Strength/heat: 5 (15,000 SHU)
Other: This is a very useful chili and its flavor is delightful. It can be eaten raw sliced in a salad, as it is quite mild. The fruit goes from green to yellow, and finishes in red. A favorite!

YAKI BLUE FAWN

Origin: Italy
Height: 3'–3¼' (90 cm.–100 cm.)
Fruit: 1⅕"–1½" (3 cm.–4 cm.) drop shape, pointed; red
Strength/heat: 10 (600,000–800,000 SHU)
Other: An ornamental chili that grows symmetrically and can become a bit tree-like. The foliage is dark and the fruit is first lilac, and then ripens to red. This one often attracts attention because its whole appearance is so aesthetically pleasing! This variety is a crossbreed with *C. chinense*, which gives it its fierce heat. This chili is also called Purple Bhut.

BERRY-STYLE PEPPERS

[CAPSICUM BACCATUM]

THIS SPECIES ORIGINATES in tropical South America, where it is called aji. Wild, closely related species are most commonly found in Bolivia and Peru, but also exist in Paraguay, northern Argentina and southern Brazil, which suggests that they were grown in this area. The name, berry-like (baccatum = berry-like) refers to the fruits, even if many cultivated varieties have oblong, smooth, and slightly knobby fruits. The flowers are white with yellow-green spots.

The species has a distinctive growth habit—there's some distance between the leaf nodes, which makes both the main and side stems long. The stems droop when they are full of fruit, which gives the plant the appearance of an umbrella. The species has periodically been called *C. pendulum* (pendant), and Carl von Linné classified it as a subspecies: *Capsicum baccatum* var. *pendulum.*

The plants grow quickly and develop a solid and sturdy stem, and can therefore become a small tree in a single season. *C. baccatum* nearly always need to be staked. Foliage varies from pale to dark green, and the leaves are unusually large, which make them vulnerable to wind damage. If the plant is grown outside, it is imperative that the spot is sheltered

SOME FACTS ABOUT BERRY-STYLE PEPPERS

Development time: 4–5 months

Sown in greenhouse: January–15th March

Strength/heat: 4–5

Other: Quick-growing species with more flavor than heat. Ripens quite early.

from the wind. Berry-like pepper is a species with very tasty fruits, which makes it perfect for the hobby grower. The species has mild heat and a delicious flavor, and ripens from green to different hues of red, orange and yellow.

Many Aji—pinkie-shaped—chilis belong to this species of pepper. Aji Amarillo, which is used in the dish ceviche, for example, is nearly the national chili of Peru. Hot Lemon is another very popular variety, which has a clear citrus note to its flavor. It is not as hot as *C. chinense* Habanero Lemon, a chili it is often mistaken for. Other common types within *C. baccatum* are the bell-shaped chilis with names such as Jamaican Bell and Bishop's Crown. The question that arises here is, how many types are there? Could it be that they are all the same variety, or are they very similar varieties that have been given different names in different parts of the world? Kerstin has found 24 different cultivars that grow into almost identical plants with the same shape of fruits, but the fruits can vary in color and heat strength. The plants are large and prolific producers.

These plants can be overwintered, but since they grow so large and bushy it's easier to sow from seed every year.

AJI AMARILLO

Origin: Peru
Height: 2'–2⅔' (60 cm.–80 cm.)
Fruit: 2¾" (7 cm.), drop shape, tapering to a point; yellow orange
Strength/heat: 7 (30,000–50,000 SHU)
Other: The name simply means yellow chili. It is used in the classic Peruvian dish ceviche, but it is also popular to dry this chili or make it into purėe.

AJI BENITO

Origin: Bolivia
Height: 3⅔' (110 cm.)
Fruit: 1½"–2" (4 cm.–5 cm.), drop shape; red
Strength/heat: 6 (15,000 SHU)
Other: This one changes from a beautiful pale green to red while it ripens. A prolific producer. A flavorful chili for those who like medium heat.

AJI CRISTAL

Origin: Chile
Height: 1⅔'–2' (50 cm.–60 cm.)
Fruit: 3⅕" (8 cm.), cone shape; red
Strength/heat: 7 (30,000–50,000 SHU)
Other: The fruit stays pale green for a long time, so it is sometimes also called Aji Blanco Cristal (or Crystal). This chili has some citrus notes and is quite meaty with a shiny, waxy skin. It is tasty even when unripe, and many prefer to eat it while it is still green.

AJI PINEAPPLE

Origin: Peru
Height: 2⅔'–3' (80 cm.–90 cm.)
Fruit: 2"–2¾" (5 cm.–7 cm.)
Strength/heat: 6 (20,000 SHU)
Other: There is a slight touch of citrus or pineapple flavor. It has a characteristic aji aroma. The fruit's appearance is similar to Hot Lemon, except that they are somewhat knobby.

AJI LITTLE FINGER

Origin: Bolivia
Height: 3¼'–4' (100 cm.–120 cm.)
Fruit: 1½" (4 cm.), dented drop shape; orange
Strength/heat: 4–5 (5,000 SHU)
Other: Funny shape that reminds you of a crooked finger, mostly a thumb. This is a very prolific producer, and the fruit is tasty. Makes a deliciously orange sauce.

AJI FANTASY

Origin: Finland
Height: 2' (60 cm.)
Fruit: 1½" wide x 2" long (4 cm. x 5 cm.), bell shape; pale yellow
Strength/heat: 7 (30,000 SHU)
Other: The Finnish breeder Jukka Kilpinen has produced a few very fine chili varieties named bell chilis. Aji White Fantasy is a mutation of Aji Fantasy, which happened at a grower's in the Canary Islands. Its color is cream, bordering on white. Sparkling is a new, even paler variety.

AJI VERDE

Origin: Peru
Height: approx. 3¼' (100 cm.)
Fruit: $2^{1}/_{3}$"–$3^{1}/_{5}$" (6 cm.–8 cm.), plump, coming to a point; red
Strength/heat: 5 (5,000–15,000 SHU)
Other: The fruit is green at first, then it turns yellow and brown and orange, until it ripens to red. It often produces many large, fine fruits.

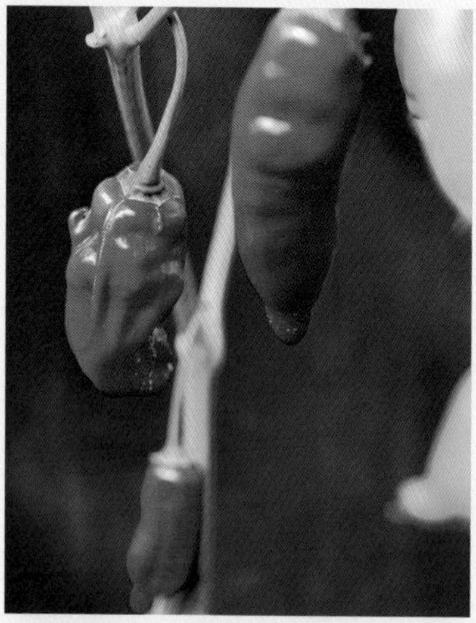

BLONDIE

Origin: Finland
Height: approx. 3¼' (100 cm.)
Fruit: $2^{1}/_{3}$"–$3^{1}/_{5}$" (6 cm.–8 cm.), oblong; white
Strength/heat: 7 (50,000 SHU)
Other: A variety that turns white or pale yellow as it ripens. Not a lot of flavor, more heat. Makes a nice dried powder. Sometimes the name is spelled Blondy.

BRAZILIAN STARFISH

Origin: Brazil
Height: 4'–5' (120 cm.–150 cm.)
Fruit: 1½" (4 cm.), saucer shape; red
Strength/heat: 8 (50,000 SHU)
Other: Grows into a small tree that branches nicely and can carry lots of fruit. The flavor is deep, full-bodied, and perfect for a variety of meat dishes. This chili freezes very well and is also good for drying.

BULGARIAN CARROT

Origin: Bulgaria
Height: 1⅓'–2' (40 cm.–60 cm.)
Fruit: 4" (10 cm.), oblong; orange
Strength/heat: 7 (30,000–50,000 SHU)
Other: This chili ripens early and yields a prolonged harvest. Grows well on a balcony and on a windowsill. In Bulgaria it is called shipkas, and it also has a nickname—Hot Carrot.

CRIOLLA SELLA

Origin: Peru/Bolivia
Height: 2'–3' (60 cm.–90 cm.)
Fruit: 2"–2¾" (5 cm.–7 cm.), drop shape; orange
Strength/heat: 9 (100,000–350,000 SHU)
Other: One of the earliest varieties to ripen. Nice fruity flavor

HOT LEMON

Origin: Peru
Height: 1⅔'–2⅔' (50 cm.–80 cm.)
Fruit: 1½" (4 cm.), oblong; pale yellow
Strength/heat: 6 (20,000 SHU)
Other: This is a very popular variety, primarily because of its citrus flavor. Rather sprawling in growth habit. It is a prolific producer, and the fruits are excellent with fish, shellfish and salads. It is also called Aji Limon and Peru Yellow. The fruit is longish and slim, a bit like a finger. This chili is often mistaken for *C. chinense* Habanero Lemon, see page 203.

INCA RED DROP

Origin: Peru
Height: 2'–2¼' (60 cm.–70 cm.)
Fruit: ¾"–1⅕" (2 cm.–3m); plump; red
Strength/heat: 5 (10,000 SHU)
Other: Very tasty, quite mild chili with a bit thicker skin walls, which means that drying takes time but it produces quite a lot of powder. The plant is often covered in fruits.

JAMAICAN BELL

Origin: Various origins; includes Brazil.
Height: 3¼'–4' (100 cm.–120 cm.)
Fruit: 1½"–2" (4 cm.–5 cm.), bell shape; red
Strength/heat: 1–2, 5–6 (approx. 1,000 SHU/15,000 SHU)
Other: A much-enjoyed variety that can grow into a small tree. It is beautiful and usually produces mild fruits. Try this: cut away the stem end, stuff the fruit with cheese, and place it on the grill! It is said that a fully developed plant can tolerate temperatures down to 41°F (5°C). We give the things we love many names, and this variety is called Patricia, Nepalese Bell, Bishop's Crown, Bishop's Hat, Joker's Hat, Bell Aji, Monk's Hat, Chapeau de Frade, Christmas Bell, and Glocken Bell Pepper. They are probably all the same variety, as their appearance is the same. However, the strength might vary between the different cultivars. Some are mild while some others are medium hot.

OMNICOLOR

Origin: Peru
Height: 2' (60 cm.)
Fruit: 2"–2¾" (5 cm.–7 cm.) narrow drop shape; red
Strength/heat: 6 (15,000–30,000 SHU)
Other: A very beautiful plant with fruit that ripens in succession; the plant can often bear green fruit as well as white, yellow, orange, and red simultaneously. Often grows into a small tree.

PERUVIAN POINTER

Origin: Peru
Height: 2'–3' (60 cm.–90 cm.)
Fruit: $2\frac{1}{3}$"–$3\frac{1}{5}$" (6 cm.–8 cm.), oblong drop shape; red
Strength/heat: 5 (10,000 SHU)
Other: Some fruit hang down while others stick straight out from the plant, or upward. Turns a beautiful orange while ripening.

RAIN FOREST

Origin: South America
Height: 3¼' (100 cm.)
Fruit: 1½" (4 cm.), round; red
Strength/heat: 5 (5,000–15,000 SHU)
Other: The fruit grow in bunches, which weigh down the branches. This one is medium hot and useful when you want a dish that is not too hot.

TREPADEIRA WERNER

Origin: Brazil
Height: $1\frac{2}{3}$'–$2\frac{2}{3}$' (50 cm.–80 cm.)
Fruit: $1\frac{1}{5}$" (3 cm.), plump drop shape; red
Strength/heat: 4 (2,500 SHU)
Other: A very prolific plant with fruit that ripen successively, which means that it has many white, pale yellow, orange, and red fruits simultaneously. The fruit contain a lot of seeds but are still good candidates for drying. You can always clean the fruit first if you don't want a lot of seeds in your powder.

HAVANA/SCOTCH BONNET PEPPERS

[C. CHINENSE]

ARE THE DIFFERENT names for this species confusing? Does the chili come from China or from Cuba? Neither! The scientific name is a mistake made by a Dutch physician at the end of the 18th century, who believed the chili originated in China, and named it accordingly. Instead, like all chilis, the species comes from South America and is very popular in the Caribbean Islands. It got its Swedish name from the Cuban capital, but also after the species' most well known variety, the habanero.

C. chinense is homogenous in its growth pattern. The plants grow quite low and compact—they're often around 1⅔'–2' (50 cm–60 cm.) tall and they're sometimes wider than they are tall. They have beautiful dark green foliage, and the leaves are slightly dented. One of their recognizable features that is common to almost all varieties is that the leaves grow in pairs with the leaves opposite each other, and the next pair of leaves grows at 90 degrees from the pair below. The plants flower abundantly, and it is not uncommon that they drop flowers due to non-pollination. Doesn't seem to matter, since a lot of fruit is still produced. These plants love heat and high humidity!

This species has many varieties, and most of them are very hot—they are often around 8–9 on the SHU, even though there are a few very mild varieties, such as Bellaforma and Habanero Apricot, for example. Apart from the heat, the varieties in *C. chinense* often have a fruity flavor that makes them very appreciated and useful in cooking, especially in different types of sauces.

Habanero Peach is one of the many habaneros. The plant has the typical growth pattern, with rather sturdy growth and slightly dented leaves.

You'll find the hottest chilis in this species, those with 10+ on the SHU. Naga Morich, Bhut Jolokia, Trinidad Moruga Scorpion, and Carolina Reaper are all *C. chinense* varieties; some even have genes from *C. frutescens.* The work of most modern breeding is mostly about finding a new hot variety that can dethrone Carolina Reaper, which has held the title of "world's hottest chili" since 2013. In New Mexico, research is at the other end of the spectrum, where they have produced milder varieties that still retain the habanero's fruity aroma. These varieties often carry the word NuMex in their names, like NuMex Suave Orange. Suave means soft/mild.

Floridians have a soft spot for the Datil habanero and they have dedicated a harvest festival to it, which is celebrated in St. Augustine every fall. This variety is also popular on the Mediterranean island of Menorca, which the inhabitants insist is its birthplace, while others maintain that the Datil comes from Cuba.

SOME FACTS ABOUT HAVANA CHILI PEPPERS

Development: 8–10 months from sowing to harvest
Sow: October–December
Strength/heat: 1–10+++; most common is 8–9
Other: These varieties are extremely flavorful and at their best when fresh. They freeze very well. Cut them into wedges if you want to dry them, and use an oven or a dehydrator because they do take time. Dried whole fruits must be cut open and checked for mold inside before they are ground into powder. Always use gloves when handling the hottest varieties. As the plants are slow to develop, it is worth the time and work spent to overwinter your favorites.

AJI CACHUCHA

Origin: Cuba
Height: 2²/₃' (80 cm.)
Fruit: 1½" (4 cm.), round with flat underside, wrinkled; red
Strength/heat: 2 (1,000–1,500 SHU)
Other: Changes from lime green to orange and then to red. That means that the fruit in the picture is not fully ripe. Sligthly wrinkled, which makes the appearance a bit like the hot Carolina Reaper, but Aji Cachucha can't boast any heat. In the West Indies it is called Aji Dulce.

AJI DULCE AMARILLO

Origin: South America
Height: 2²/₃' (80 cm.)
Fruit: 1½" (4 cm.), round; orange yellow
Strength/heat: 1 (1,000 SHU)
Other: Dulce means sweet, which is a good description of the longer, oblong Aji Amarillo's cousin. The chili has a very fruity and nice aroma, and the foliage smells good as well.

AJI LLANERO

Origin: Venezuela
Height: 1²/₃' (50 cm.)
Fruit: 2¹/₃"–2¾" (6 cm.–7 cm.), plump with ridges; red
Strength/heat: 3 (1,500 SHU)
Other: The mild heat supports its good flavor very well.

AJI PANCA

Origin: Peru
Height: 3'–3¼' (90 cm–100 cm.)
Fruit: 2¾"–4" (7 cm.–10 cm.), oblong, dented; brown
Strength/heat: 1 (500–1,000 SHU)
Other: A very mild but very flavorful chili with big fruits; very nice for stir-fries and to use as a side dish. It's used for Mexican mole sauce.

BHUT JOLOKIA

This variety has its origin in northeastern India and is grown primarily in the states of Assam, Arunachal Pradesh, Nagaland, and Manipur. These are the hottest chilis in the world and measure more than 1 million SHU. Scientists have found traces of *C. frutescens* when they studied the DNA of Bhut Jolokia, which means that the chili is a cross; however, it is closer to *C. chinense*. The fruits are dented and drop-shaped, usually red but other colors exist. Jolokia is spelled Zôlôkiya, which is the Indian name for capsicum. Bhut or bih, its other name, means poison, which alludes to the enormous strength of the heat. They are also called Naga chilis or ghost peppers. Naga is Sanskrit for cobra. Naga is associated with fertility and wealth, and pictures of snakes are used in religious ceremonies to cure infertility.

BHUT JOLOKIA PEACH

Origin: India
Height: 3' (90 cm.)
Fruit: 1½"–2" (4 cm.–5 cm.), plump, drop shape; apricot color
Strength/heat: 10+ (800,000–1,000,000 SHU)
Other: A variety of Bhut Jolokia that changes from green to apricot color when ripe.

BHUT JOLOKIA STRAIN II

Origin: India
Height: 3'–3¼' (90 cm.–100 cm.)
Fruit: 1½"–2" (4 cm.–5 cm.), drop shape ending in a point, wrinkled; red
Strength/heat: 10+ (800,000–1,000,000 SHU)
Other: One of the world's top ten hottest chili varieties. It is also called Bhut Jolokia Improved Strain II. We've been informed that its heat can exceed 1 million Scoville.

BHUT JOLOKIA WHITE

Origin: India
Height: 2¼' (70 cm.)
Fruit: 1½"–2" (4 cm.–5 cm.), plump, ending in a point; white
Strength/heat: 10+ (900,000 SHU)
Other: A really hot chili! Beautiful ripening process from green to beige, over peach color to nearly completely white. This one is perfect if you want white chili powder. This chili is also called White Naga or Ghost Pepper White.

BIG BLACK DEVIL

Origin: Bangladesh
Height: 3' (90 cm.)
Fruit: 2"–$2\frac{1}{3}$" (5 cm.–6 cm.), unevenly round, rugged-looking and wrinkled; brown
Strength/heat: 10 (350,000–800,000 SHU)
Other: An unusual variety that is beautiful with its dark fruits and its greenish lilac foliage. A very hot and prolific variety.

BROWN BHUTLAH

Origin: Canary Islands
Height: $3\frac{1}{4}$' (100 cm.)
Fruit: $3\frac{1}{5}$"–$3\frac{1}{2}$" (8 cm.–9 cm.), drop shape with a "waist," wrinkled; reddish brown
Strength/heat: 9 (100,000–350,000 SHU)
Other: Bred in the Canary Islands by crossing Trinidad Douglah and Bhut Jolokia

BUT ORANGE COPENHAGEN

Origin: Denmark
Height: $2\frac{2}{3}$'–3' (80 cm–90 cm.)
Fruit: 2"–$3\frac{1}{5}$" (5 cm.–8 cm.)
Strength/heat: 10+ (800,000–1,000,000 SHU)
Other: Bred by Sören Friis Larsen in Denmark. The name is commonly shortened to BOC by the initiated. Extremely hot!

CAJA VERMELHA

Origin: Brazil
Height: $2\frac{2}{3}$' (80 cm.)
Fruit: $\frac{3}{4}$"–$1\frac{1}{5}$" (2 cm.–3 cm.), plum shape; red
Strength/heat: 7 (40,000 SHU)
Other: Smooth fruits that have a fresh and nice flavor that goes well in salads.

CAJAMARCA

Origin: Peru
Height: 2'–3' (60 cm–90 cm.)
Fruit: 2¾"–3$^{1}/_{5}$" (7 cm.–8 cm.), oblong; red
Strength/heat: 6 (15,000–30,000 SHU)
Other: Beautiful, bushy plant with lots of fruit that change from green to beige, lilac and red. Useful variety with very good flavor, and this is one of Kerstin's favorites that she often uses when cooking.

CARBONERA

Origin: Florida
Height: 2¼'–2$^{2}/_{3}$' (70 cm.–80 cm.)
Fruit: 2$^{1}/_{3}$" (6 cm.), uneven shape; orange
Strength/heat: 9 (100,000–350,000 SHU)
Other: A quite new variety that is a cross between Habanero Orange and Carbon Bhut 7 Pot. Fruit and heat in the same bite. This one is also called Orange Carbonero. Sometimes classified under *Capsicum annuum*.

CGN 21566

Origin: Brazil
Height: 3' (90 cm.)
Fruit: 1½" (4 cm.), slim, UFO shape; yellow orange
Strength/heat: 9 (150,000 SHU)
Other: A distinctly different plant with dark lilac, almost black foliage. The fruit also has an odd shape, and ripens to yellow.

CAROLINA REAPER

Origin: South Carolina
Height: 3¼'–5' (100 cm.–150 cm.)
Fruit: 1½"–2⅓" (4 cm.–6 cm.), uneven cone shape, wrinkled; red
Strength/heat: 10+++ (1,569,383–2,200,200 SHU)
Other: In 2013 this chili was named the world's hottest chili; the record still stood as of 2017. It is a cross between Sweet Habanero and Naga Viper. The variety was originally called HP22BNH7. Like many other superhot chilis, it has a sting growing on the fruit. The fruit can be used in sauces and as a powder. Extremely hot even when eaten raw! Use gloves when you touch the fruit. It's not for nothing that it's called the "Reaper."

CGN 23209

Origin: Honduras
Height: 3' (90 cm.)
Fruit: 2"–2¾" (5 cm.–7 cm.), oblong; brown-black
Strength/heat: 6 (15,000–30,000 SHU)
Other: A tall, slender plant with fruits that turn a delicious brown black when ripe.

CHEIRO ROXA

Origin: Brazil
Height: 2¼'–3' (70 cm.–90 cm.)
Fruit: ¾"–1⅕" (2 cm.–3 cm.), plump drop shape; rose lilac
Strength/heat: 8 (60,000 SHU)
Other: An attractive plant that's well worth growing for its decorative touch. Switches between hues of lilac and pink.

CRIOLLA DE COCINA

Origin: Nicaragua
Height: 2¼' (70 cm.)
Fruit: 2"–2⅓" (5 cm.–6 cm.), round with deep ridges; red
Strength/heat: 3–4 (1,500–5,000 SHU)
Other: This chili ripens early. It has very thin skin, so if you hold it against the light you can see straight through the fruit and make out the inside. A good candidate for drying.

DEVIL'S RIB

Origin: Ghana
Height: 4' (120 cm.)
Fruit: 2"–2¾" (5 cm.–7 cm.), spool shape with shallow ridges; red
Strength/heat: 10 (400,000 SHU)
Other: Maybe it's the ribs that are protruding on this beautiful fruit; however, it does have a lot of heat and bites "like the devil!"

DORSET NAGA

Origin: England
Height: 5' (150 cm.)
Fruit: 2" (5 cm.), drop shape with shallow ridges; red
Strength/heat: 10+ (1000,000–1,100,000 SHU)
Other: Dorset Naga is developed from Ghost Pepper (Bhut Jolokia), and is related to Naga Morich. Good in sauces and spice mixes. It is excellent to dry and to grind into powder. This chili is so prolific that a British seed company holds the Dorset Naga Challenge competition every year to see who can grow the most fruits.

ECUADORIAN BROWN

Origin: Ecuador
Height: 3¼' (100 cm.)
Fruit: $3\frac{1}{5}$"–3½" (8 cm.–9 cm.), oblong, drop shape; brown
Strength/heat: 8 (50,000–100,000 SHU)
Other: Beautiful big fruits in brown black on a quite slender plant.

FATALII RED

Origin: Africa
Height: 2¼'–$2\frac{2}{3}$' (70 cm.–80 cm.)
Fruit: 2" (5 cm.), drop shape ending in a point; red
Strength/heat: 10 (500,000 SHU)
Other: There are several Fatalii that are similar both in appearance and taste. The red one is a bit hotter. It doesn't always grow completely true and might ripen to yellow. The white variety is called Fatalii White and the yellow, Fatalii Yellow.

FIDALGO ROXA

Origin: Brazil
Height: 2¼' (70 cm.)
Fruit: 1$^{1}/_{5}$" (3 cm.), "Barbapapa"*, "candy floss" shape; rosy lilac
Strength/heat: 8 (50,000–100,000 SHU)
Other: An odd shape and a very beautiful color, almost morello-cherry lilac red. Dark green foliage turns to lilac.

GEORGIA BLACK

Origin: Venezuela
Height: 4' (120 cm.).
Fruit: 2$^{1}/_{3}$"–3$^{1}/_{5}$" (6 cm.–8 cm.), oblong; brown
Strength/heat: 6 (15,000–30,000 SHU)
Other: Tall slender plant with fruit changing colors directly from green to brown. The fruity flavor comes through nicely because the heat is not overpowering.

*after the title character Barbapapa (Candy floss) in a French children's book.

HABANERO

Habanero, which means "from Havana," is the name attached to the species *Capsicum chinense*. Habanero is also the collective name of a large group of chili fruits. Habanero was first discovered in Yucatán in Mexico, and probably originated in Peru. This chili is very popular, and is where many varieties in the West Indies come from, which is evident from names like Habanero Guadeloupe. As a rule, the fruits have a very special shape, plump with four deep "ridges," like a small apple. However, there are also small round fruits, some of which are shaped like Halloween pumpkins. The colors of ripe fruits vary from near white to apricot, red, orange, yellow, brown, and purple. The typical habanero flavor is fruity. They are generally very hot, around 100,000 and 500,000 SHU, but there are milder varieties that are below 1,000 SHU. The English name for habanero is Scotch Bonnet. Typically the varieties have heat and flavor in common, but their appearance varies.

HABANERO APRICOT

Origin: West Indies
Height: 2'–3' (60 cm.–90 cm.)
Fruit: 1½"–2" (4 cm.–5 cm.), a bit slimmer than most habaneros; dark apricot
Strength/heat: 1 (100–1,000 SHU)
Other: Very beautiful apricot-colored fruit and one of the mildest habanero varieties, it still has the same good fruitiness of other habaneros. Enjoyed by those who want the flavor but milder heat.

HABANERO BELLAFORMA

Origin: Trinidad and Tobago
Height: 2'–2¼' (60 cm.–70 cm.)
Fruit: 1¹/₅"–2¹/₃" (3 cm.–6 cm.), drop shape with ridges; red
Strength/heat: 1 (700 SHU)
Other: This one has the habanero's good fruity flavor without almost any heat. It is perfect for anyone who does not want a hot chili but seeks the habanero flavor anyway.

HABANERO BIG SUN

Origin: Africa
Height: 2'–3' (60 cm.–90 cm.)
Fruit: 1½"–2" (4 cm.–5 cm.), plump to drop shape; orange
Strength/heat: 9 (350,000 SHU)
Other: Orange yellow habanero with typical appearance, somewhat more pointy toward the end. Fruity and tasty and very hot.

HABANERO BLACK

Origin: West Indies
Height: 2'–3' (60 cm.–90 cm.)
Fruit: 1½" (4 cm.), plump with ridges; black
Strength/heat: 9 (300,000 SHU)
Other: This fruit has exceptionally deep ridges, and its color is a deep burgundy, as close to black as you can get. The fruit is very beautiful and has a fruity flavor with lots of heat. This is also called Black Habanero.

HABANERO BROWN

Origin: West Indies
Height: 2'–3' (60 cm.–90 cm.)
Fruit: 1½"–2" (4 cm.–5 cm.), plump with ridges; brown
Strength/heat: 9 (100,000–350,000 SHU)
Other: Beautiful chocolate brown habanero that is very prolific. Somewhat smoother-skinned fruit than most habaneros. Fruity and tasty and very hot.

HABANERO CARIBBEAN RED

Origin: Mexico
Height: 2'–3' (60 cm.–90 cm.)
Fruit: 1½"–2" (4 cm.–5 cm.), plump with a faint touch of habanero ridges; red
Strength/heat: 10 (475,000 SHU)
Other: A fruity and tasty habanero with lots of flavor and heat. It changes from pale green to orange and red. This one is also called Antillais Caribbean.

HABANERO CONGO ORANGE

Origin: West Indies
Height: 2⅔'–3¼' (80 cm.–100 cm.)
Fruit: 1⅕"–1½" (3 cm.–4 cm.), plump ending in a small point; orange
Strength/heat: 10 (300,000–577,000 SHU)
Other: A big chili plant of the habanero variety that grows a bit wider than most *C. chinense*.

HABANERO DATIL

Origin: Florida
Height: 2'–3' (60 cm–90 cm.)
Fruit: 1½"–2" (4 cm.–5 cm.), drop shape; yellow orange
Strength/heat: 9 (100,000–300,000 SHU)
Other: A small habanero chili. The flat leaves make one suspect a cross with another species. Nice sweetness and heat. A Datil Pepper Fall Festival is celebrated in Florida every fall.

HABANERO EBONY GIANT

Origin: West Indies
Height: 2'–3' (60 cm.–90 cm.)
Fruit: $2^1/_3$"–2¾" (6 cm.–7 cm.), plump with ridges; brown-red
Strength/heat: 9 (100,000–350,000 SHU)
Other: Dark wine red, almost brown fruit with an obvious habanero shape. Fruity and hot. Somewhat tree-like in growth habit.

HABANERO GAMBIA ORANGE

Origin: Gambia
Height: 3' (90 cm.)
Fruit: 2"–$2^1/_3$" (5 cm.–6 cm.), plump and blunt; orange
Strength/heat: 6 (30,000 SHU)
Other: A sweet and hot habanero from Africa.

HABANERO GAMBIA RED

Origin: Gambia
Height: 2'–3' (60 cm–90 cm.)
Fruit: 1½"–2" (4 cm.–5 cm.), plump; red
Strength/heat: 6 (15,000–30,000 SHU)
Other: Prolific habanero chili that produces green, orange, and red fruits all at the same time. This chili is very decorative. Mild to medium heat.

HABANERO GOLDEN

Origin: Caribbean
Height: 2'–3' (60 cm.–90 cm.)
Fruit: 1½"–2" (4 cm.–5 cm.), plump drop shape; orange
Strength/heat: 9 (150,000–350,000 SHU)
Other: Golden yellow habanero with strong ridges.

HABANERO GUADELOUPE

Origin: Guadeloupe
Height: 2'–3' (60 cm.–90 cm.)
Fruit: 2"–2⅓" (5 cm.–6 cm.), plump with ridges; red
Strength/heat: 9 (200,000 SHU)
Other: A classically shaped habanero with fruit that changes from green to orange, and ends in red.

HABANERO HAROLD'S ST. BART

Origin: Saint-Barthelemy
Height: 2'–3' (60 cm–90 cm.)
Fruit: 1½"–2" (4 cm.–5 cm.), plump with ridges; yellow orange
Strength/heat: 9 (100,000–350,000 SHU)
Other: This chili comes from the former Swedish colony of Saint-Barthelemy—commonly called St. Barts—in the Antilles archipelago in the West Indies.

HABANERO LARANJADA GRANDE

Origin: Brazil
Height: 2'–2¼' (60 cm.–70 cm.)
Fruit: 1¹/₅"–1½" (3 cm.–4 cm.), plum shape; cream-colored to white
Strength/heat: 9 (300,000 SHU)
Other: This plant is often loaded down with many fruits that have a beautiful white hue and attractive shape.

HABANERO LEMON

Origin: West Indies
Height: 1²/₃' (50 cm.)
Fruit: 1¹/₅"–1½" (3 cm.–4 cm.), drop shape; yellow
Strength/heat: 9 (200,000–350,000 SHU)
Other: A popular chili with lemon flavor. The lemon is not quite as obvious as with *C. baccatum* Hot Lemon because the Habanero Lemon is hotter and the heat overpowers the flavor. These two chilis and their names are often confused, but there is no variety called Habanero Hot Lemon. Habanero Lemon is sometimes called Lemon Drop because of its appearance.

HABANERO MUSTARD

Origin: The Caribbean
Height: 2'–2²/₃' (60 cm.–80 cm.)
Fruit: 1½"–2" (4 cm.–5 cm.), plump with deep ridges; brown-orange
Strength/heat: 9 (150,000–350,000 SHU)
Other: The chili gets its name from the fruit's mustard color, and has nothing to do with its flavor.

HABANERO NARANJA PICANTE

Origin: West Indies
Height: 2'–2²/₃' (60 cm–80 cm.)
Fruit: 1½"–2" (4 cm.–5 cm.), drop shape with ridges; orange-yellow
Strength/heat: 10++ (1,100,000 SHU)
Other: It's common that the fruits differ in shape, sometimes plump drop shapes, at other times more classical habanero shapes with deep ridges. The fruit is fiery hot and the whole plant gives off a nice orange scent.

HABANERO NATAL

Origin: Brazil
Height: 1²/₃'–2' (50 cm.–60 cm.)
Fruit: ¾" (2 cm.), round; red
Strength/heat: 9 (100,000–350,000 SHU)
Other: A beautiful plant with dark foliage. It is classified as a habanero, but the leaves make you suspect a cross with *C. annuum*. The chili has a very tasty, fruity flavor reminiscent of apricot. The entire plant emits a delicious scent. The fruits often ripen in different stages, turning to lilac, yellow, orange, and red simultaneously.

HABANERO ORANGE

Origin: Mexico
Height: 2'–2²/₃' (60 cm.–80 cm.)
Fruit: 1½"–2¹/₃" (4 cm.–6 cm.), plump with ridges; yellow-orange
Strength/heat: 9 (100,000–350,000 SHU)
Other: A typical habanero with beautiful color and good flavor. This one is also called Habanero Orange Devil.

HABANERO PASTEL

Origin: West Indies
Height: $2\frac{1}{4}$' (70 cm.)
Fruit: $1\frac{1}{5}$"–$1\frac{1}{2}$" (3 cm.–4 cm.), plump with ridges; peach-colored
Strength/heat: 9 (100,000–350,000 SHU)
Other: Sometimes confused with Habanero Peach, this one is even more peach-colored, while Peach is more on the beige side. A very prolific plant. When dried, the fruit makes a very beautiful pale beige powder.

HABANERO PEACH

Origin: West Indies
Height: 2¼' (70 cm.)
Fruit: 1 1/5" (3 cm.), plump with ridges; peach-colored
Strength/heat: 9 (150,000–350,000 SHU)
Other: A very tasty and beautiful fruit with an unusual color.

HABANERO PI 281429

Origin: Surinam
Height: 3'–3½' (90 cm.–110 cm.)
Fruit: 1½"–2 1/3" (4 cm.–6 cm.), plump; apricot color
Strength/heat: 10 (580,000 SHU)
Other: PI is the abbreviation for Plant Inventory, and it was registered with the USDA in 1962. The plant is originally from Surinam and is recognized as an heirloom. An extremely unusual plant.

HABANERO PURPLE

Height: 2'–3' (60 cm.–90 cm.)
Fruit: 2"–2 1/3" (5 cm.–6 cm.), round with deep ridges; reddish brown
Strength/heat: 8 (50,000–100,000 SHU)
Other: A popular chili with beautiful fruits that range from lime green to reddish brown when ripe. Its name is misleading, because the fruit isn't purple.

HABANERO RED

Origin: Mexico
Height: 2'–2 2/3' (60 cm.–80 cm.)
Fruit: 1½"–2" (4 cm.–5 cm.), plump with ridges; bright red
Strength/heat: 9 (325,000 SHU)
Other: A classic habanero in bright red with deep beautiful ridges. Substantial strength and rounded flavor with fruity notes are other characteristics. The first fruits of the harvest might be a bit smoother, but keep harvesting and the larger typical fruits will arrive eventually. This chili is known by many names, and there are similarities with Umba as well as Caribbean Red. This chili is referred to as Scotch Bonnet in English-speaking countries.

HABANERO UMBA

Height: 2'–3' (60 cm–90 cm.)
Fruit: 1½"–2' (4 cm.–5 cm.), plump with a "waist" and ridges; red
Strength/heat: 9 (100,000 -350,000 SHU)
Other: Another red habanero with a lot of similarities to the regular Habanero Red. However, it differs a bit in its shape. It is also called Aji Umba and Aji Umba Red.

HABANERO WHITE GIANT

Origin: Caribbean
Height: 2⅔'–3' (80 cm.–90 cm.)
Fruit: 2" (5 cm.), plump with deep ridges; white
Strength/heat: 9 (300,000 SHU)
Other: Beautiful fruits in a lime green hue that changes to white—the closer to ripe it is, the lighter the color. It keeps its color well when dried.

HABANERO YELLOW

Origin: West Indies
Height: 2'–3' (60 cm.–90 cm.)
Fruit: 2" (5 cm.), drop shape; yellow
Strength/heat: 9 (300,000 SHU)
Other: The plant is so prolific that the branches are weighed down with fruit, and the whole plant gets a droopy look.

HABANERO YELLOW BUMPY

Height: 2⅔'–3' (80 cm–90 cm.)
Fruit: 1⅕" = 1½" (3 cm.–4 cm.), teacup saucer shape; orange-yellow
Strength/heat: 9 (300,000 SHU)
Other: This chili produces fruits that are wider than long; they are about 2" (5 cm.) wide and 1⅕"–1½" (3 cm.–4 cm.) long.

PIMENTA PINGO DE OURO

Origin: Brazil
Height: 3'–5' (90 cm.–150 cm.)
Fruit: 1/3"–½" (1 cm.–1 ½ cm.), pea shape; orange
Strength/heat: 9 (100,000–350,000 SHU)
Other: A very tall and slender plant with the tiniest fruits, which still makes for a very attractive ensemble: the fruits make the whole plant look like it's covered in golden balls—the name means golden drop. Fiery and tasty habanero flavor.

SCOTCH BONNET FOODORAMA

Origin: Texas
Height: 3½' (110 cm.)
Fruit: 2"–2⅓" (5 cm.–6 cm.), plump with ridges; orange
Strength/heat: 9 (100,000–350,000 SHU)
Other: This one is reminiscent of other Scotch Bonnets; it's both fruity and hot. Wide plant with long side branches.

HOT PAPER LANTERN

Height: 2¼' (70 cm.)
Fruit: 2¾" (7 cm.), drop shape; red
Strength/heat: 9 (150,000–350,000 SHU)
Other: A fine chili with a nice growth habit and beautiful red fruits.

JAMAICAN RED

Origin: Jamaica
Height: 2' (60 cm.)
Fruit: 2" (5 cm.), plump with ridges; red
Strength/heat: 8 (50,000–100,000 SHU)
Other: This plant yields a lot of fruit and substantial heat. It is similar to a Habanero Red but doesn't have the same fruitiness.

JAMAICAN YELLOW

Origin: Jamaica
Height: 2' (60 cm.)
Fruit: 1½"–2¾" (4 cm.–7 cm.), plump with ridges; yellow-orange
Strength/heat: 9 (150,000 SHU)
Other: Produces many big yellow fruits with the characteristic habanero appearance of deep ridges. The leaves are typical for a *C. annuum*, so this chili might be the result of a cross. Beautiful, hot, and tasty.

JELLYBEAN

Origin: Peru
Height: 2¼'–3' (70 cm–90 cm.)
Fruit: $\frac{1}{3}$"–¾" (1 cm.–2 cm.), egg shape; whitish yellow
Strength/heat: 4 (2,500–5,000 SHU)
Other: The plant produces lots of small white fruits, each and every one of which is loaded with seeds. As the heat is moderate, this chili is good in salads or to eat fresh in some other way. This one also goes by the name Yellow Fire.

MADAME JEANETTE

Origin: Surinam
Height: 2$\frac{2}{3}$' (80 cm.)
Fruit: 1½"–2$\frac{1}{3}$" (4 cm.–6 cm.), plump with ridges; yellow orange
Strength/heat: 8 (100,000 SHU)
Other: A prolific plant, even though it might be a bit difficult to get it to start growing. The fruits are the habanero type both in appearance and flavor. This one is also called Surinam Yellow.

MOJO SCOUNDREL

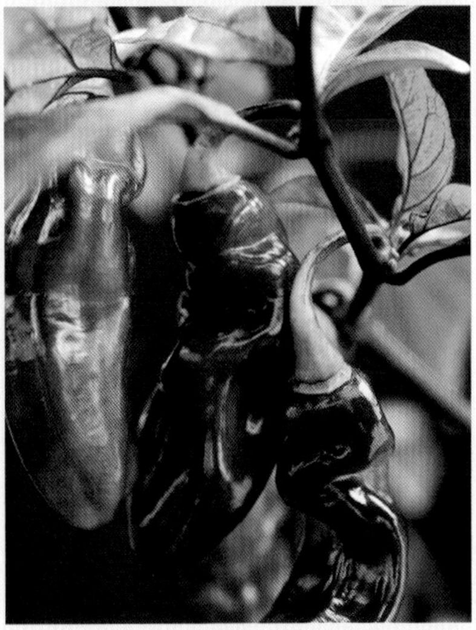

Origin: Italy
Height: 2¼' (70 cm.)
Fruit: 1½"–2" (4 cm.–5 cm.), dented drop shape; different lilac hues
Strength/heat: 10 (350,000–800,000 SHU)
Other: Scoundrel means crook, and this one has a little bit of a roguish appearance. The fruits aren't conforming but change appearance. The fruits are meant to be dark lilac, but can turn out pale lilac/beige.

NAGA MORICH

Origin: Bangladesh
Height: 1⅔'–2' (50 cm–60 cm.)
Fruit: 2" (5 cm.), wrinkly drop shape; red
Strength/heat: 10+ (1,000,000–1,100,000 SHU)
Other: The heat does not make it inedible, even though it scores a 10. Do taste it! However, it isn't quite as tasty as Naga Morich Chocolate.

NAGA MORICH CHOCOLATE

Origin: Bangladesh
Height: 1⅔'–2' (50 cm.–60 cm.)
Fruit: 2" (5 cm.), plump drop shape; brown
Strength/heat: 10+ (800,000–1,000,000 SHU)
Other: A very prolific plant, and a variety you can eat fresh even though it is hot. It is especially tasty when semi-dried (a bit like a sun-dried tomato). This chili can be eaten as candy! It is also called Big Bang Naga.

NUMEX SUAVE RED

Origin: New Mexico
Height: 2¼'–3' (70 cm.–90 cm.)
Fruit: 2" (5 cm.), plump with ridges; red
Strength/heat: 2 (1,000–1,500 SHU)
Other: The NuMex varieties are bred by the Chile Pepper Institute at New Mexico State University, and they have succeeded in cross-breeding habanero and producing a much milder fruit that kept its fruitiness. Super tasty fruity flavor that is absolutely delicious fresh. There is even an orange: NuMex Suave Orange.

PIMENTA PUMA

Origin: Italy
Height: 2⅔'–3¼' (80 cm.–100 cm.)
Fruit: 1⅕"–1½" (3 cm.–4 cm.), oblong, sometimes with ridges; brown-orange
Strength/heat: 7 (30,000–50,000 SHU)
Other: A chili with a very unusual color; maybe we could say it's pumpkin-colored. The fruits vary quite a lot, as the plants don't always come in true. Dark foliage.

PIMENTA DA NEYDE

Origin: Brazil
Height: 4¼' (130 cm.)
Fruit: 1½"–2" (4 cm.–5 cm.), plump; black-lilac
Strength/heat: 9 (100,000 SHU)
Other: This is the blackest of the chilis, and it stays black. An older plant can be completely black: stem, foliage, and fruit. This chili is often used in crossbreeding to arrive at other black-lilac varieties.

PINK TIGER

Origin: Italy
Height: 2'–2¼' (60 cm.–70 cm.)
Fruit: 2¾"–3 1/5" (7 cm.–8 cm.), drop shape, dented; lilac—sometimes stripy
Strength/heat: 10 (350,000–800,000 SHU)
Other: This one's picture is usually shown when it has lilac stripes on its beige or pale pink skin, but these stripes have a tendency to disappear as the fruit ripens. The color variation shows that there are traces of the dark Pimenta de Neyde present in the genes. This chili is quite rare, and when it was introduced its seeds were the most expensive in the world—they could cost around $10 each.

PURPLE PEACH

Origin: Mexico
Height: 2' (60 cm.)
Fruit: 1 1/5" (3 cm.), spherical shape; peach color with lilac streaks
Strength/heat: 5 (15,000 SHU)
Other: This is an ornamental chili that is extremely decorative. Dark foliage edging into black with many small beautiful fruits.

SANTA ROSA BLANCO

Origin: Peru
Height: 2¼'–3' (70 cm.–90 cm.)
Fruit: 1 1/5" (3 cm.), plump drop shape; white
Strength/heat: 10 (500,000 SHU)
Other: This one can look very innocent but it stings like a bee! Small, beautiful fruit with a sting at the end of body, and fierce heat. Changes to lilac before ripening, and the nodes on the stem are also beautifully lilac-colored. This chili is also sold as Santa Rosa Blanca.

SCARLET LANTERN

Origin: Peru
Height: 2'–3' (60 cm–90 cm.)
Fruit: 1½"–2" (4 cm.–5 cm.), drop shape, somewhat slimmer at the stem end; red
Strength/heat: 9 (300,000 SHU)
Other: Gorgeous fruits, which really earn their name as the many fruits shine like lanterns in yellow, orange, and red.

SCOTCH BONNET CHOCOLATE

Origin: Jamaica
Height: 2'–3' (60 cm.–90 cm.)
Fruit: 1½"–2" (4 cm.–5 cm.), plump with ridges; brown
Strength/heat: 9 (350,000 SHU)
Other: Habanero chilis are called Scotch Bonnets in English-speaking countries, so it isn't always easy to know whether it is a true variety or just another name for habanero. Good fruity flavor and fierce heat. This one comes in red and yellow, too.

TOBAGO SEASONING

Origin: Trinidad and Tobago
Height: 3' (90 cm.)
Fruit: 1⅕"–2" (3 cm.–5 cm.), plump drop shape, some ridging; red
Strength/heat: 4 (2,500–5,000 SHU)
Other: Nice plant with fine fruit, good habanero flavor and quite mild.

TRINIDAD SCORPION

These varieties originated in the Moruga region of Trinidad and Tobago. Trinidad Moruga Scorpion is bred by agriculturist Wahid Ogeer. Trinidad Moruga Scorpion was named the world's hottest chili in 2012, a record it kept only for a few months. Since that year several more chilis with identical heat levels have appeared. Trinidad Scorpion Butch x Pot Jonah has also held the world record. The hot fruits have a fruity flavor that makes them much loved.

TRINIDAD 7 POT RED

Origin: Trinidad and Tobago
Height: 2'–3' (60 cm.–90 cm.)
Fruit: 2"–2¾" (5 cm.–7 cm.), round and wrinkled with a sting at the end; red
Strength/heat: 10+ (800,000–1,000,000 SHU)
Other: One of the really fiercely hot chilis that burn your mouth! It is difficult to experience anything but heat when you bite into this one. It is typically wrinkled, like many of the fiercely hot 7 Pot varieties from Trinidad and Tobago. There is also a white version with the name 7 Pot White.

TRINIDAD MORUGA SCORPION

Origin: Trinidad and Tobago
Height: 2⅔'–3¼' (80 cm.–100 cm.)
Fruit: 2⅓"–2¾" (6 cm.–7 cm.), plump and pointed, wrinkled with sting at the end; red
Heat: 10++ (1,200,000–2,009,231 SHU)
Other: The typical shape and wrinkles warn of extreme heat. TMS, as it is called by its fans, was voted the world's hottest chili in 2012.

TRINIDAD MORUGA SCORPION YELLOW

Origin: Trinidad and Tobago
Height: 2'–2²/₃' (60 cm.–80 cm.)
Fruit: 2" (5 cm.), plump drop shape with sting at the end; yellow
Heat: 10++ (1,200,000–2,009,231)
Other: One of the world's hottest chilis, which of course competed for the world title, presenting a single fruit measuring more than 2,000,000 SHU. A beautiful fruit for which you need to use gloves even just picking it off the plant. This one is also called Trinidad Scorpion Cardi Yellow because it was bred at the Caribbean Agricultural Research and Development Institute, in Cardi.

TRINIDAD SCORPION BUTCH T

Origin: US
Height: 3¼' (100 cm.)
Fruit: 1½"–2" (4 cm.–5 cm.), drop shape, wrinkled with a sting at the end; red
Strength/heat: 10+++ (1,463,700 SHU)
Other: Bred by Butch Taylor in Mississippi. Blushes beautifully from the stem end and downward. Classic shape, wrinkled and with a sting at the end, just like a scorpion will have. To have such a specific Scoville level means that the fruit has been laboratory-tested and has vied for the designation of world's hottest chili—a title it won in 2011.

TRINIDAD SCORPION BUTCH T X POT JONAH

Origin: USA
Height: 2'–2²/₃' (60 cm.–80 cm.)
Fruit: 1½"–2" (4 cm.–5 cm.), plump drop shape with sting at the end; red
Strength/heat: 10++ (1,200,000 SHU)
Other: One of the superhot crosses that has held the title of world's hottest chili. Check out the sting at the end, which is typical for these varieties. The "x" in the name means that it is a cross between the two varieties. This chili is also called Trinidad 7 Pot Jonah. Add an entire fruit to a stew, and remove it once it has given off enough heat so it doesn't overpower the dish.

TRINITY

Origin: Mexico
Height: 2'–3' (60 cm.–90 cm.)
Fruit: 2¹/₃" (6 cm.), drop shape; red
Heat: 7 (40,000 SHU)
Other: Shiny red fruits with beautiful shape. The heat can sometimes get even stronger.

TABASCO PEPPERS

[CAPSICUM FRUTESCENS]

TABASCO ISN'T JUST a Mexican state but also a world-famous hot sauce, and the state has also given its name to this species of *Capsicum.* This is quite a small group, Tabasco and Piri Piri being the most recognizable. Piri Piri (which is actually PiliPili, if we are to be correct) means both chili and pepper in Swahili.

C. frutescens is one of the first species that Linné described, and he named it after its growth habit (*frutescens* = bushlike). The growth is quite dense and it has small, thin leaves in a beautiful green hue. The species grows wild in the Amazon River's delta, in Colombia and in Peru. It likes both heat and high humidity but isn't very picky about windy conditions. Its condensed growth habit makes it perfect as a potted plant. If you bring it inside in the fall it can make a very decorative houseplant, even as a Christmas plant if the red fruits are left on. This species probably spread westward, with birds or seafarers, from South America to Asia, before the 16th century.

Its flowers' color can vary from white to yellow and lilac, and not just between different varieties but also on the same bush. The Tabasco plant is one of the varieties in which the flower colors vary. The fruits are small and narrow and often grow upright, but some varieties have hanging fruits. They are red or yellow when ripe, with a rather neutral flavor and a moderate but distinct heat.

Tabasco chili is of course indispensible for the classic American sauce Tabasco, but even the people of Angola and Mozambique have welcomed this chili into their kitchens and hearts. Lemon, onion, and bell pepper are other ingredients in the Piri Piri sauce that is commonly served in South Africa. The leaves from the Siling Labuyo variety are used in *tinola*, a chicken stew; *sambal oelek*, an Indonesian sauce, is also originally made from *C. frutenscens*

The plants overwinter very well if you have the space for them, but you can also sow them from seed each year.

SOME FACTS ABOUT TABASCO PEPPERS

Development: 4–7 months, depending on the species
Sow: January–February
Strength/heat: 10,000–300,000 SHU
Other: Usually yields lots of small fruits that are easy to dry, even at room temperature, since their skin is so thin.

Piri Piri

AFRICAN RED DEVIL

Origin: Africa
Height: $1^{1}/_{3}$' (40 cm.)
Fruit: $1^{1}/_{5}$"–¾" (3 cm.–4 cm.), spool shape; red
Strength/Heat: 8 (50,000–100,000 SHU)
Other: It will be covered with small, hot fruits. It makes a good potted plant for the balcony or deck. This is sold as a variety of Piri Piri, and the fruits are similar, but not in growing habit.

BANGKOK UPRIGHT

Origin: Thailand
Height: 3' (90 cm.)
Fruit: 2"–2 1/3" (5 cm.–6 cm.), narrow with a blunt end; red
Heat: 6 (15,000–30,000 SHU)
Other: This is a Thai chili; the fruit grows upward, which gives the plant a slightly funny appearance. There's a slight bitterness in the flavor, which a Thai chili should have to balance out the Thai dishes. This one is sometimes classified with *C. annuum.*

MALAWI BIRDSEYE

Origin: Africa
Height: 9¾"–1 1/3' (25 cm.–40 cm.)
Fruit: ¾"–1 1/5" (2 cm.–3 cm.), plump drop shape; red
Strength/Heat: 9 (200,000 SHU)
Other: Very good, fruity flavor with substantial heat. It's a beautiful plant with pendant growth habit. Looks good in a hanging basket or as a houseplant. This chili is popular in countries like Malawi, Zambia, Ghana and Nigeria. It grows wild in the African landscape. The fruit is used in nali hot sauce.

NEPAL SNAKE BITE

Origin: Nepal
Height: 2 2/3' (80 cm.)
Fruit: 6"–approx. 7" (15 cm.–18 cm.), oblong; red
Strength/Heat: 5 (10,000 SHU)
Other: A beautiful plant with many fruits that turn counterclockwise, which adds an extra dimension to its appearance.

PERUVIAN PURPLE

Origin: Peru
Height: 2' (60 cm.)
Fruit: ¾"–1⅕" (2 cm.–3 cm.), egg shape; red
Strength/Heat: 6 (15,000–30,000 SHU)
Other: A decorative plant where the foliage and fruits can be completely black-lilac, and the fruit ripens to red.

PIRI PIRI

Origin: Mozambique/Angola
Height: 2⅔'–3' (80 cm.–90 cm.)
Fruit: 1½" = 2" (4 cm.–5 cm.), oblong; red
Strength/Heat: 7–9 (30,000–300,000 SHU)
Other: Very popular all over South Africa. Its heat depends on the seed's origin, and it can go from quite mild to blisteringly hot. There are many chili varieties called Piri Piri—this isn't so strange, since it is the African name for chili.

TABASCO

Origin: Mexico
Height: 2'–2⅔' (60 cm.–80 cm.)
Fruit: 1⅕"–1½" (3 cm.–4 cm.), drop shape; red
Strength/Heat: 7 (30,000–50,000 SHU)
Other: This chili is named after the Mexican state Tabasco, and is known for the sauce of the same name. The flavor of the sauce has very little in common with the flavor of the fresh fruit. The sauce is fermented, which gives it a completely different taste. This is a fantastically beautiful plant, with fruits that ripen from green to yellow and then to red, so the plant very often displays three colors of fruit simultaneously.

ROCOTO PEPPERS

[CAPSICUM PUBESCENS]

THIS SPECIES CAME originally from Bolivia, in the area around the Andes. A scientific description of the Rocoto emerged quite late—1794—and it has very little genetic variations. Rocoto is the least common of the five species, with few cultivars. It differs substantially from the other four well-known species, and it's impossible to crossbreed Rocoto with the others to generate new varieties. Scientists believe that Rocoto is closely related to wild species like *Capsicum eximium* and *C. cardenasii,* because they have found spontaneous crossbreeding between these species and *C. pubescens.*

Today, Rocoto chilis can be found in all the countries around the Andes, like in Peru, Chile, and Colombia. It is grown commercially primarily in this region, but can also be found in Central America up to Mexico.

Commercial growing is concentrated primarily to the Andes area because the fruits don't keep as long as other chili fruits—the Rocoto is a lot fruitier and will start going moldy faster, which shortens their shelf life in grocery stores. But it also requires specific growing conditions. *Capsicum pubescens* demands a longer season than other species, with a warm and humid summer climate coupled with cooler periods. As this chili comes from the highlands where the winters can turn cold, an established plant that has collected a lot of strength over the long warm summer might survive a light frost. You can overwinter these plants in a screened-in porch or greenhouse where an electronic frost guard ensures the temperature stays around 50°F (10°C) during the day, and never dips below 41°F (5°C). They overwinter very well indoors, preferably with extra growth light, or else on a windowsill.

The name *pubescens* refers to the fact that the plant is hairy. *Pubes* means scant hair growth or "covered in down," and this is a clear, recognizable sign. It actually shows as soon as the plants emerge from the soil!

Their growth habit is often bushy, and a plant grows often as much in width as in height—it can end up being 1⅓' tall and 5' wide. In the rainforest, its natural habitat, the plant's outstretched branches can hook on to other vegetation and kind of haul itself up toward the light. Under optimal growing conditions, the plant can reach a height of many feet and live for over 10 years. Many who grow Rocoto peppers in pots train their pepper plants on supports to save space, and also to help the plant bear its many heavy fruits. The Rocoto pepper is more shade tolerant than other chilis; it even likes the shade, which means that it can be placed in a more shaded area of the greenhouse.

Another of the Rocoto pepper's recognizable features is its large leaves. They are spaced far apart and smell heavenly. Many Rocoto peppers develop large lilac flowers with yellow spots, but there are also ones that have white flowers, often with a touch of lilac.

The fruits are mostly round as apples, often golf ball sized, but there are varieties that are more plum-shaped and smaller, sized more like a cherry. "Rocoto Longo," the jalapeño-shaped variety, is grown commercially in the Canary Islands. Ripe fruits are red, yellow, or brown. The Rocoto pepper is the meatiest of all chili species, with juice and flavorful flesh that are similar to the bell pepper in texture. They are also very hot, but their fruitiness makes the heat seem milder than the hot varieties in, say, *Capsicum chinense.*

Only this species has black seeds. If there is any uncertainty about the species, its dark seeds will be stronger proof than anything whether it is a C. pubescens or not. The seeds keep their dark color when dried.

The Rocoto pepper goes by different names depending on where in the world it grows. The indigenous population of the Andes highlands called this chili fruit *locoto,* which becomes *rocoto* in Spanish. Rocoto peppers with yellow fruits are sometimes called *canario,* which refers to their color. In Guatemala the pepper is sometimes called *caballo* (horse) because the people say that it kicks like a horse. The name *manzano,* which means apple tree, is common in Mexico.

SOME FACTS ABOUT ROCOTO PEPPER

Development: 8–10 months
Sow: October–November
Strength/heat: 7–9 (30,000–00,000 SHU)
Other: The Rocoto pepper is best eaten fresh, but can also be frozen. If you want to dry it, it is best to cut it into wedges and dry it in the oven or in a dehydrator, because the drying time is so lengthy.
It is an advantage if you can overwinter the plant, as its development takes so long. Plant height refers to freely growing plants. The plant can reach more than 3¼' (1 meter) in height if it is trained.

BROWN ROCOTO

Origin: Bolivia
Height: 1'–$1\frac{2}{3}$' (30 cm.–50 cm.)
Fruit: $2\frac{3}{4}$"–$3\frac{1}{5}$" (7 cm.–8 cm.), sphere shape; brown
Strength/heat: 7 (30,000–50,000 SHU)
Other: The fruit changes from green to brown and stays brown.

CHRISTOBAL COLOMBO

Origin: South America
Height: 3¼' (100 cm.)
Fruit: 2" (5 cm.), blunt, oblong; yellow
Strength/heat: 7 (30,000–50,000 SHU)
Other: Beautiful dark yellow and juicy fruit. The shape is more oblong than most of the other Rocoto chilis.

COSTA RICAN YELLOW

Origin: South America
Height: 2¼'–2⅔' (70 cm.–80 cm.)
Fruit: 2" (5 cm.) egg shape; yellow
Strength/heat: 9 (100,000–350,000 SHU)
Other: This classic Rocoto chili has a beautiful yellow color. The variety also exists in red, Costa Rican Red.

ROCOTO GRANDIS

Origin: South America
Height: approx. 1⅔' (approx. 50 cm.)
Fruit: 2⅓"–3⅕" (6 cm.–8 cm.), sphere shape; red
Strength/heat: 9 (300,000 SHU)
Other: A very juicy and tasty fruit, with substantial heat. Suitable for eating fresh in small bites, despite its heat. Has beautiful lilac flowers.

ROCOTO PERU

Origin: Peru
Height: 1'–1⅔' (30 cm.–50 cm.)
Fruit: 1⅕"–1½" (3 cm.–4 cm.)
Strength/heat: 7 (30,000–50,000 SHU)
Other: Kerstin just got this plant. A friend brought it back after a trip to Peru to visit a friend. The flavor is very similar to Rocoto Grandis, but the fruit is smaller and more egg shaped. Kerstin named the fruit herself.

ABOUT THE AUTHORS

Eva Robild is a garden journalist and author of more than 20 books. Eva is also an editor for Swedish Television's *Trädgårdstider* (Garden Times).

Kerstin Rosengren grows 300 varieties of chilis at Himlabacken, her home on Österlen, where she works as a textile artist.

Pernilla Bergdahl is an experienced garden photographer who works for Swedish and international publications. She has contributed to several gardening books.

THANK YOU!

BIG thank-yous go to Anders Larson for his encouragement, his help with trundling stuff around, and not to mention his all-around assistance during the long photo shoots at Himlabacken.

. . . and to Linda Grundsten for the Chili Paté recipe, and Helena Svensson for the Habanero Salsa recipe! Last but not least, a BIG thank-you to Gösta Christiansson at Sneckenström Ekohandel for information about neem cake and fertilizing.

SOURCES

BOOKS

Borssén, Rabén. *Eat the Heat.* Prisma, 1996.

Dewitt, Dave, and Paul W. Bosland. The Complete Chili Pepper Book. Timber Press, 2009

RESEARCH

Coon, Danise, Eric Votava, and Paul W. Bosland *The Chile Cultivars of New Mexico State University Released from 1913 to 2008.* New Mexico State University Research Report 763, 2008

Eshbaugh, W. Hardy. "Peppers: History and Exploitation of a Serendipitous New Crop Discovery." In J. Janick and J. E. Simon (eds.), *New Crops.* New York: Wiley, 1993.

"Hot Pepper Compound Inhibits Growth of Breast Cancer Cells." Sci-News, December 22, 2016.

Kraft, Kraig H. et al. "Multiple Lines of Evidence for the Origin of Domesticated Chili Pepper, Capsicum annuum, in Mexico. Proceeding of the National Academy of Sciences of the United States of America 111(17): 6165–70, April 29, 2014.

Perry, L., et al. "Starch Fossils and the Domestication and Dispersal of Chili Peppers (Capsicum spp. L) in the Americas." Science 315(5814):986–8, February 16, 2007.

WEB PAGES

Chiliplanet.eu

Dave's Garden, davesgarden.com

Guinness World Records, guinnessworldrecords.com/

Jalapeno.nu

Läkemedelsverket, lakemedelsverket.se

Nationalencyklopedin.ne.se

New Mexico State University, Chile Pepper Institute, cpi.nmsu.edu/

Örtagårdens plantskola, ortagarden.com

Puckerbutt Pepper Company, puckerbuttpeppercompany.com/

Svensk kulturväxtdatabas, slu.se/centrumbildningar-och-projekt/skud

Svenska Chilipepparföreningen, chilepeppar.com

MAGAZINE ARTICLES

Bergstrand, Karl-Johan. "Växter växer bäst i vitt ljus." *Natur & Trädgård* 4, 2014.

Bradford, Amanda. "Love Your Enchiladas? You Can Thank NMSU Chile Research Pioneer Fabian Garcia." New Mexico State University News Center, August 1, 2016.

Chen, Angela. "Why Do We Like Hot Peppers?" *The Verge.* September 17, 2016.

Falk, Barbro. "Chili kan bli medicin." *Allergia.* October 21, 2016.

Green, Barry. "Why Is It That Eating Spicy, 'Hot' Food Causes the Same Physical Reactions As Does Physical Heat (Burning and Sweating, for Instance)?" *Scientific American.* October 21, 1999.

"Hemliga tricket bakom Clintons uthållighet." *Tidningarnas Telegrambyrå.* March 10, 2013.

Nilsson, Johan. "Brännhet läkemedelsforskning." *Vetenskapshälsa. March 23,* 2015.

Robinson, Simon. "Chili Peppers: Global Warming." *Time. June 14,* 2007.

Rydén, Daniel. "En rymdresa släcker chilins eld." *Helsingborgs Dagblad.* July 24, 2016.

INDEX

Notes

Notes

Notes

Notes

Notes

First published by Bonnier Fakta, Stockholm, Sweden

10 9 8 7 6 5 4 3 2

Library of Congress Cataloging-in-Publication Data is available on file.

Cover design by Qualcom
Cover photo by Pernilla Bergdahl

Print ISBN: 978-1-5107-4037-2
Ebook ISBN: 978-1-5107-4038-9

Printed in China